Physical Characteristics of the German Pinscher

W9-ANY-121

(from the American Kennel Club breed standard)

Back: Short, firm and level.

Topline: The withers form the highest point of the topline, which slopes slightly toward the rear, extending in a straight line from behind the withers, through the well-muscled loin to the faintly curved croup.

Loin: Well muscled.

Body: Compact and strong, so as to permit greater flexibility and agility.

Hindquarters: The thighs are strongly muscled and in balance with forequarters. The stifles are well bent and well boned, with good angulation.

Size: The ideal height at the highest point of the withers for a dog or bitch is 17–20 inches.

Coat: Short and dense, smooth and close lying. Shiny and covers the body without bald spots.

Feet: Short, round, compact with firm dark pads and dark nails. The toes are well closed and arched like cat feet.

German Pinscher

By Sharon Morgan with
Dee Gannon

Contents

Training Your German Pinscher   92

Begin with the basics of training the puppy and adult dog. Learn the principles of house-training the German Pinscher, including the use of crates and basic scent instincts. Enter puppy kindergarten, introduce the pup to his collar and leash and progress to the basic commands. Find out about obedience classes and other activities.

Healthcare of Your German Pinscher   109

By Lowell Ackerman DVM, DACVD
Become your dog's healthcare advocate and a well-educated canine keeper. Select a skilled and able veterinarian. Discuss pet insurance, vaccinations and infectious diseases, the neuter/spay decision and a sensible, effective plan for parasite control, including fleas, ticks and worms.

Showing Your German Pinscher   134

Step into the center ring and find out about the world of showing pure-bred dogs. Here's how to get started in AKC shows, how they are organized and what's required for your dog to become a champion. Also take a leap into the realms of obedience and agility trials and tracking tests.

Behavior of Your German Pinscher   146

Analyze the canine mind to understand what makes your German Pinscher tick. Issues discussed include different types of aggression, separation anxiety, sex-related behaviors, chewing, digging and jumping up.

KENNEL CLUB BOOKS® GERMAN PINSCHER
ISBN: 1-59378-355-8

Copyright © 2007 • Kennel Club Books, LLC • 308 Main Street, Allenhurst, NJ 07711 USA
Cover Design Patented: US 6,435,559 B2 • Printed in South Korea

Library of Congress Cataloging-in-Publication Data
Morgan, Sharon.
  German pinscher / by Sharon Morgan and Dee Gannon.
    p. cm.
  1. German pinscher. I. Gannon, Dee. II. Title.
SF429.G367M67 2007
636.73--dc22   2006016292

10 9 8 7 6 5 4 3 2 1

Photography by:

Ashbey Photography, Paulette Braun, Carolina Biological Supply, Fritz Clark/
The Standard Image, Juliette Cunliffe, Tom Digiacomo, Phyllis Ensley/Pet Action Shots,
Isabelle Français, Bruce Harkins, JC Photo, Carol Ann Johnson, Bill Jonas, Dr. Dennis Kunkel,
Bill Meyer, Tam C. Nguyen, Tom and Linda Nutting/A-N Productions, Phototake,
Jean Claude Revy, Rubin, David Sombach Photography, Tattle Tail Pet Photography,
Michael Trafford, Tom Weigand and Julie Williams.

Illustrations by Patricia Peters.

Not a miniature Doberaman Pinscher, the German Pinscher is actually a forebear of his larger Doberman relative and is closely related to the Standard Schnauzer.

HISTORY OF THE

GERMAN PINSCHER

"From time immemorial, a typical kind of dog shared the life of the southern German rural population. The species was about nineteen inches tall, had a smooth or wiry coat of an inconspicuous color ranging from brown over gray to black. Known as the *benchur* or *rattenfanger*, they were mainly used as watchdogs and vermin killers in and around the homesteads. From this primal stock, modern cynology has developed well-defined pinschers and schnauzers of different sizes, coats and colors."

John Gallant
The World of the Schnauzers

It is generally accepted that the German Pinscher and the Standard Schnauzer owe their origins to the common farm dog known as the Rattler that had become firmly established in Germany in the 15th century. These dogs were used to guard the farm and to kill vermin. They came in two varieties: the rough-coated and the smooth-coated. The smooth-coated variety is most likely the ancestor of the German

HARLEQUIN PINSCHER

An extinct cousin of the German Pinscher is the Harlequin Pinscher, recognized by the Reichsverband fur das Deutsche Hundewesen (RDH), the governing canine agency in Germany, in the 1920s and accepted for showing by the Fédération Cynologique Internationale. The breed was distinguished for its harlequin coloration, described in the standard as "spotted grey, or black, or dark on a white or clear ground, with or without tan markings." The coat was short and shiny, like that of the Pinscher, and the dog was square in build yet still elegant. The breed had the same alert, lively character that makes the German Pinscher so desirable, described in the standard as "roguish and attentive." In size, the Harlequin Pinscher stood 17 to 19 inches (43 to 48 centimeters), the same size as the German standard for the Pinscher today.

Pinscher. The smooth-coated pinscher is also credited as being one of the ancestors of the Doberman Pinscher, which began to be developed in Germany in the 1890s. The rough-coated variety eventually developed into the Standard Schnauzer.

While there are a variety of references in the writings of the early and mid-19th century to both the rough- and the smooth-coated pinscher-type dogs, it was not until 1880 that the first breed standard for the pinscher was written. Allowed colors included rust-yellow, gray-yellow, black, iron-gray, silver-gray, flax-blonde, dim gray-white and white with gray dappling.

In 1895 Josef Berta founded the first Pinscher Club in Germany to register both the smooth- and rough-coated pinschers. During the ensuing years, the smooth-coated pinscher was all but forgotten amid his rough-coated counterparts. The few smooths that were registered came primarily from litters produced by rough parents. Despite their low numbers, Josef Berta insisted that the smooth-coated pinscher continue to be registered and exhibited.

In 1907 Dr. Zurhellen founded the Bayrischen Schnauzerklub in Munich. In 1918 Berta and Zurhellen merged the two clubs to form the Pinscher-Schnauzer-Klub, which exists to this day. This joint organization divided the pinscher population into six distinct breeds, which are the Affenpinscher, Miniature

Pinscher, German Pinscher, Miniature Schnauzer, Standard Schnauzer and Giant Schnauzer. In the first joint stud book published in late 1925, litters and individuals of both pinscher and schnauzer breeds were listed. As time went on, records were kept of breedings, and, after three generations of producing a specific type of dog, individual registrations were issued by breed name.

The first German Pinscher registered by breed name in the Pinscher-Schnauzer-Klub stud book was Alexius Schnauzerlust, who was whelped on June 24, 1917. He was salt and pepper in color, as were numerous others subsequently registered. Finally, in 1923, the breed standard for the German Pinscher was reviewed and changed in order to encourage the breeding of the German Pinscher. Allowed colors were bright red, red/brown to dark red/brown, black with red markings, yellow or red/yellow in various tones and salt and pepper in various tones without any rust coloring. The breed was being forced to stand on its own, and only in rare cases were the smooth-coated offspring of one or more Schnauzer parents registered.

In the early history of the German Pinscher, there were other pinscher types similar to the German Pinscher that appeared or were created. Of the first registered German Pinschers in Germany, a number were salt and pepper in color. This color was sustained by the Pinscher-Schnauzer-Klub into the 1930s, but most of the German Pinscher breeders felt that this color was too close to the Schnauzer and have not produced this color for

DOBERMAN RELATIONS

Although not nearly as popular as his larger cousin, the German Pinscher is the forerunner of the Doberman Pinscher. While Herr Louis Dobermann used several different breeds to create the Doberman, his breeding program originated with his two Pinschers, Schnupp and Bisart. At the turn of the 20th century, a breeder named Herr Goller was offering for sale a new breed, the Doberman Pinscher. He wrote of this new breed that he was convinced that it had sprung from crosses between the Thuringian German Shepherd, the smooth-haired Pointer, the blue Great Dane and, most significantly, the German smooth-haired Pinscher.

A PINCH OF SALT AND PEPPER
The popular coloration in the schnauzer breeds, salt/pepper, is not permitted in the German Pinscher today, though in the early part of the 20th century it was tolerated. The salt/pepper coloration was only permitted when the dogs were bred out in this color for at least three generations, which is to say that they were not smooth versions of the ever-popular Standard Schnauzer of this color.

many decades. During the 1930s and 1940s, Dr. Dauber produced a number of solid black German Pinschers. His breedings were the only ones ever entered into the stud books and none has been registered since the early 1940s.

Following World War II, the German Pinscher almost declined into extinction. No German Pinscher litters were registered in West Germany between the years 1949 and 1958. The few German Pinschers that remained were rapidly aging beyond their ability to reproduce. Werner Jung, the breed warden for the Pinscher-Schnauzer-Klub, stated publicly that the club had neglected the breed to the point of extinction and that nobody seemed to care. Jung then abandoned his 25 years of work with the Giant Schnauzer to take on the revitalization of the German Pinscher breed.

While the German Pinscher was dying out in West Germany, several litters a year were still being registered in East Germany. In 1957 Jung was fortunate to acquire a pure-bred bitch from one of these litters. Kitti v. Boestrand Bsg was black with red markings. She was not regarded as the best example for breeding but was adequate as a starting point. Jutta Jung, a pinscher-type black bitch that has been described as an oversized Miniature Pinscher, was also selected and registered with the Pinscher-Schnauzer-Klub as German Pinscher foundation stock. There were no pure-bred German Pinscher males available, but there were males of the pinscher type that could be used to recreate the German Pinscher. Jung carefully selected three oversized Miniature Pinscher males. These were Illo Fischer (black), Fuerst Jung (red) and Onzo Ilgen (bronze or chocolate).

Jung decided to create two

bloodlines: one line from Jutta Jung and the other line from Kitti v. Boestrand Bsg. The offspring were then interbred as Jung moved forward with revitalizing the German Pinscher. From 1958 through 1968, Jung produced 34 litters for a total of 158 puppies. Most, if not all, of the German Pinschers today trace their ancestry back to these five dogs.

In 1960 three German Pinschers were awarded the title of Bundesseiger, and four others were rated excellent at the Frankfurt-am-Main show. At this point, it was said that Jung had succeeded in bringing the German Pinscher back from the brink of extinction. Today the German Pinscher is well established worldwide and is easily identifiable.

The Fédération Cynologique Internationale (FCI) recognized the German Pinscher in 1957. The FCI standard was prepared in conjunction with the Pinscher-Schnauzer-Klub. Most other countries have used the FCI standard as the basis for drafting their own standards according to the requirements imposed by their individual kennel clubs. While many countries are affiliated with the FCI, there are some such as the United States, Great Britain, Canada and Japan that are independent organizations and accept breeds on an individual basis. The Kennel Club of Great Britain recognized the German Pinscher in 1988. The United Kennel Club (UKC), the second largest American all-breed registry, recognized the breed as part of the Terrier Group in 1991.

ANCIENT ORIGINS

Of the five types of dog identified from fossil remains from about 4500 BC, the Pinscher most likely evolved from a spitz-type dog. This Peat or Lake Dog, found in Switzerland, Germany, eastern and northern Europe is thought to be the ancestor of the modern-day Spitz dogs, like the Pomeranian, German Spitz and American Eskimo. A form of these dogs, with a more capacious and lighter cranium, a less pointed muzzle and a moderately strong bite, is said to have further developed into the pinscher, schnauzer and terrier types of dog and were found spread widely throughout Europe.

The Canadian Kennel Club (CKC) recognized the breed as part of the Non-Sporting Group in 2000. The American Kennel Club (AKC), the main registering body in the US, recognized the breed as a member of the Working Group in 2003.

THE GERMAN PINSCHER IN THE UNITED STATES

The German Pinscher is still a relatively young breed in the United States. The first German Pinscher entered into the German Pinscher Club of America's stud books was Basko v. Warturm, a black and tan male imported from Germany in 1982 by Mike and Maryanne Mueller. At approximately the same time, they imported an older black and red female named Cendi v. Rednitzgrund.

> **SCHNAUZER CROSS**
>
> In 1923 no more interbreeding between the Schnauzer and Pinscher was allowed by the German Pinscher-Schnauzer-Klub. However, because of concern about the limitations of the gene pool, a small group of dedicated breeders in Finland campaigned for many years to be able to crossbreed once more with the Standard Schnauzer. This was finally allowed in the late 1990s, and about three litters of three different schnauzer/red pinscher crosses have been born. Finally the offspring of these litters will be mated together. After three generations the resulting litters will, once more, be allowed to be registered as pure-bred Pinschers.

In early 1983 Dr. J.C. Roby of Whitesville, Kentucky imported a pair of German Pinschers named Larry v. Munchhof and Mary v. Munchhof. A little later, Natalie Berman of Columbus, Georgia returned from Germany with a pair of German Pinschers from the Vogelweide kennel. Vogelweide was the kennel prefix for Josef Berta.

In 1988 Kristin Dedich purchased Wiener Kindl Bambina, a red bitch, from Austria. Bambina had been bred to Demon Z Pyselky, an International, Polish, Hungarian, Austrian and CSSR champion before being imported into the US. On July 20, 1988 a litter of six was whelped.

Taking the world by storm, here is Int. Ch. Jambo de la Capelliere. Photo by Bruce Harkins.

There were three reds and three black and tans in the litter. These were the first red German Pinschers born in the US. Kismet's Red Falcon, author Sharon Morgan's first German Pinscher, came from this litter as did Kismet's Kaiser Wilhelm and Kismet's Sir Toby. All of these dogs had a significant impact on the German Pinscher in the country in the early 1990s.

In 1992 Robin Vuillermet of Des Charmettes kennel began importing German Pinschers from France. This French influence is still seen in many of the German Pinschers today, especially those that originate from the Windamir Des Charmettes breeding program.

Since then, there have been German Pinschers imported from Austria, Australia, the Czech Republic, Finland, France, Germany, Great Britain, Holland and Sweden.

After its arrival in the US, the German Pinscher first became part of the rare-breed community while working toward AKC recognition. Rare-breed shows provided a showcase for newly imported breeds. The recognition of the German Pinscher as a strong conformation competitor that consistently dominated the Working Group at rare-breed shows encouraged the breeders to excel further in developing top-quality German Pinschers. The versatility and trainability of the

Michael Mueller became the first person to import a German Pinscher to the US when he brought over this black and red bitch, Cendi v. Rednitzgrund.

breed drew the obedience and other performance-event enthusiasts. In addition, those who liked the look of the Doberman but wanted a smaller dog for apartment/condominium living were drawn to the German Pinscher. Over the years, the

The first dual-titled German Pinscher in the US following AKC recognition, here is Ch. LaZar Des Charmettes CD. He was also the first US-born German Pinscher to win the World Championship title, which he did a record six times.

German Pinscher slowly but surely has developed a strong following. During its time as a "rare breed," the German Pinscher consistently dominated the show ring.

In April 1991, one month after the UKC admitted the breed into its Terrier Group, the American German Pinscher Breeders Association (AGPBA) became the UKC's parent club.

The German Pinscher Club of America (GPCA) was founded by a small group of breed enthusiasts in California in 1985. The purpose of the GPCA was to advance and promote the breed in the United States. Mike Mueller was the first GPCA president. From 1986 through 1990, the driving force behind the GPCA was Roger Brasier and Dianna Jones.

The GPCA held its first national specialty in 1991 in Columbus, Ohio. The first national specialty winner was Scootamore's Far to Go, an import from Gloria Cuthbert's kennel in Great Britain.

The door to AKC-licensed performance events was opened when the German Pinscher was admitted into the Miscellaneous Class in 2001. The following year the AKC recognized the GPCA as the official AKC parent club. Finally, the German Pinscher was admitted into the AKC's Working Group in January 2003, thus making the breed eligible for AKC championships and its attendant annual awards. The entry into the AKC conformation ring had been long anticipated, so many fanciers were anxious to succeed with their fully recognized Pinschers.

The first AKC champion, Ch. Riward's Rollin' Rocs Rusty, earned his title on January 8, 2003. Then, on April 20, 2003, Rusty became the

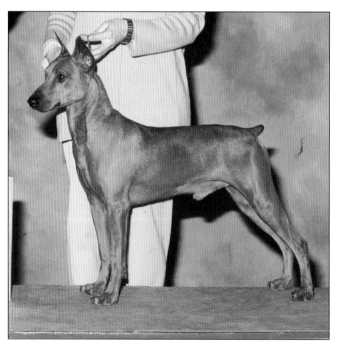

Ch. Windamir's Siam Des Charmettes was the first Best of Breed at the GPCA national specialty following AKC recognition.

WHAT'S IN A NAME?

The word *pinscher* in German simply means "terrier," though it likely derived from the Middle English and Anglo French. It has been said that the breed gained its unprepossessing name because of the dog's habit, when both playing and catching small vermin, of gripping (or pinching) the toy or prey with his two front legs. *Pinscher* also means the "grabber" or "gripper." Although some countries still call the dogs German, Standard or Medium Pinscher, the breed is known as Pinscher most commonly throughout the world now. The UK and Norway changed their breed name to Pinscher as recently as the year 2000. In the US, the breed remains known as the German Pinscher.

Following a year of great excitement in the conformation ring, the German Pinscher qualified for the 2003 AKC/Eukanuba National Championship in December 2003, held in Long Beach, California. The Best of Breed winner was Ch. Windamir Roi Des Charmettes, a lovely black and rust male owned by the author, Robin Vuillermet and Kathy Dorwart. During the first year, Roi attained the status of the number-one German Pinscher.

Then came the German Pinscher's first Westminster

This is Kismet's Red Falcon, owned by Sharon Morgan. He is the first obedience-titled German Pinscher in the US as well as the only three-time national specialty (AGPBA) winner.

first German Pinscher to place first in the Working Group. Rusty is a red male owned by Anne Richardson of Florida and was bred by author Sharon Morgan and Rita Salins.

The first dual-titled German Pinscher was Ch. LaZar Des Charmettes CD, bred by Robin Vuillermet and owned by Sharon Morgan and Kathy Dorwart.

The first GPCA national specialty following AKC recognition was held at the Kennel Club of Philadelphia on November 15, 2003. Best of Breed was awarded to Ch. Windamir's Siam Des Charmettes, a beautiful dark red male owned by Robin Vuillermet and Sharon Morgan.

Windamir Sophia Des Charmettes is the first female to earn an AKC championship.

First AKC champion fawn Ch. Windamir's Sahara B, handled by author Sharon Morgan.

Kennel Club show in February 2004, where Best of Breed was awarded to Ch. Windamir's Hunter Des Charmettes, a black and rust male owned by the author, Robin Vuillermet, Kathy Dorwart and Cynthia Dubusc. Hunter was ably handled by Mr. Daniel Rosa, who was Windamir Des Charmettes' primary handler while the dogs were being shown in the rare-breed shows and at the annual World Dog Show competitions sponsored by the FCI. Best of Opposite Sex went to Ch. Windamir's Chosen One (Zen), owned by Joelle and Tanya Kaminski. This was especially thrilling as Zen was their first show dog.

The German Pinscher also excelled at performance events. The first AKC obedience titlist was Ch. Windamir's Hunter, a LaZar son. Hunter was the first German Pinscher to earn the Companion Dog (CD), Companion Dog Excellent (CDX) and

COLORS IN THE PINSCHER

The Pinscher has, in the past, been found in a wide variety of colors. Originally in the German standard, the preferred color was black with yellow/brown markings, with darker markings preferred. Not preferred were brown dogs with yellow markings, yellow dogs or yellow/red dogs. White was never tolerated. Later colors mentioned were black/tan, pepper/salt (Schnauzer influence), brown, black and blue/tan. By 1957 the colors given in the breed standard were black/tan (with the more tan the better), solid black, roe-buck brown to stag red, brown, chocolate, blue-gray with red/yellow markings and silver-gray. Strongly disapproved were bright yellow and Isabella (fawn). Today, in most countries the only colors allowed are black/tan and various shades of red. In only a handful of countries are blue/tan and fawn tolerated. Interestingly, it is only within the last few years that the red color has been allowed in the Pinschers of the Czech Republic.

Ch. Windamir Roi Des Charmettes is the first German Pinscher to attain the ranking of number-one AKC German Pinscher.

Utility Dog (UD) titles in AKC obedience. He is owned by Georgia Welch.

The first AKC agility titlist was Ch. Blue Banners High Noon CD, AXP, AJP, owned by Betsy Spilis, who called him "Shooter." What Shooter started, many others have followed. The German Pinscher is a regular participant in agility trials.

The first AKC rally titlist was Windamir's Olga Des Charmettes RN, a black and tan female owned by Tanya Kaminski of Toledo, Ohio. Olga was Tanya's first German Pinscher.

The first AKC tracking titlist was Lankers A Black Wind Rising CD, TD, a black and tan female owned by Elizabeth White of Oregon.

The GPCA was accepted as an AKC member club in October 2005, and Robin Vuillermet became the club's first AKC delegate.

GERMAN PINSCHER

PHYSICAL CHARACTERISTICS

The German Pinscher is a medium-sized dog, measuring 17 to 20 inches at the shoulder. The size range applies equally to both sexes. He is a substantial dog with a square build. The well-balanced, flowing outline of the German Pinscher gives a definite impression of elegance.

In appearance, there are two types of German Pinscher. These are referred to as the Schnauzer-type and the Doberman-type. The Schnauzer-type is heavier boned and squarer in build. The head is stronger and broader. The Doberman-type is somewhat lighter in bone and has a more refined appearance to the head. This type is usually leggier than the Schnauzer-type.

There is no preference given between the two types, but conformation judges tend to prefer one to the other depending upon their background in dogs. The German Pinscher Club of America regularly presents breed seminars throughout the United States to continue to educate conformation judges about the finer points of the breed.

PERSONALITY

The German Pinscher is an excellent guardian and companion. He is alert and intelligent. He has

> ### NOT A WATER DOG
> Most (but not all) Pinschers have a complete and utter dislike of water in any form. They really need great encouragement to venture forth (for what a dog must do) when it is raining hard. They totally dislike getting their paws wet and will even jump or skirt around puddles when out on a walk. Bathing is something they will tolerate only because it pleases you.

Kind and affectionate, brave and intelligent, the German Pinscher will be a welcomed treasure to the right family.

highly developed senses and a fearless attitude while being devoted to his family.

The German Pinscher can be very affectionate and loves being a member of the family. This, combined with a somewhat independent nature, makes the breed especially fascinating. Each German Pinscher is unique in his attitude and approach to life.

The German Pinscher is boldly inquisitive. He keeps an eye on his surroundings at all times. He may play with a single toy for hours or seek a different one every few minutes. Some German Pinschers treasure their toys and have them for years, while others shred them as soon as they can. Balls are especially attractive and entertaining for the German Pinscher and owner alike. The jumping ability of the German Pinscher is astounding, being able to jump 3 to 4 feet into the air from a standing position. Some German Pinschers have even shown an

The German Pinscher will be bold and assertive but will also be a loving and devoted companion. This is Riward's Black Diamond, commonly known as "Solo," at 19 months.

affinity for water and love swimming in pools, charging in and out of the ocean and playing with a garden hose. They can act like clowns and entertain their owners for hours on end.

German Pinschers are quick and agile. They delight in a good run with their owner. That same quickness can result in a loose dog that no one can catch. They do not have handles. The musculature and smooth coat do not provide any places on the dog's anatomy that the human pursuer can grab onto and retrieve the dog without a collar and a leash. No one can outrun a

CANDID CAMERA

Many people are confused about the Pinscher's ability to actually smile. They will complain that the dog is baring his teeth menacingly at them. They fail to notice that this so-called "snarling" is usually accompanied by vigorous tail wagging. The Pinscher tends to use his smile when you have chided him and he actually grins, broadly, at you to get back on your good side.

Have dog, will travel! Your German Pinscher is inquisitive and will enjoy new environments to investigate.

German Pinscher. This alone lends credence to the breeder's directives that obedience training the German Pinscher is a must.

German Pinschers can become quite serious and intent when there is a mouse to catch or backyard vermin to locate. They will dig deep to locate a yard mole or chew through walls for that ever-so-elusive mouse. They make very warm sleeping companions and love to burrow under the bed covers with their owners.

Before deciding if the German Pinscher is the breed for you and your family, it is important that you understand the breed's behavior. The German Pinscher is not a breed for everyone. They require the firm hand of an experienced dog person, preferably someone with experience with the working and/or terrier breeds. This is not a good first breed for the inexperienced or the timid.

WHAT HE'S LIKE TO LIVE WITH

A German Pinscher wants to be your buddy. He likes to be part of the family and to go places with you. He has a high energy level; this is a very busy breed. The German Pinscher finds each and every new environment fascinating and will check it out again and again. He has an excellent nose and is a skilled hunter.

The German Pinscher takes pain very seriously and is most likely to snap or bite when someone hurts him. He tends to protect first and think about it later. This is why the

A NEW BABY IN THE HOUSE

Pinschers are extremely possessive and can be jealous of any seeming usurper of their family's affection. There have been cases where the sudden introduction of a new baby has caused problems, with the dog snarling and growling at the baby. This can be overcome by remembering not to neglect and seemingly ignore your Pinscher now that you have a new baby. The Pinscher is extremely possessive of his humans, and this situation handled correctly will actually make him protective of the baby, but he must never feel usurped by the newcomer.

German Pinscher is not good with young children. He has a hard time telling the difference between a real problem and good old-fashioned roughhousing. A small child who is running and screaming will set off the German Pinscher. In addition, a young child is more likely to hurt a German Pinscher than an older child. The German Pinscher is not a forgiving dog. He will forever remember someone who has hurt him.

German Pinschers can be good companions for older children as long as they are raised with them. It is always recommended that families with children get a puppy. An adult German Pinscher that has not been raised with children is unlikely to adapt well. While some breeders will not sell German Pinschers to families with children, the author not only has raised her own son with them but also has successfully sent many German Pinscher pups to grow up with children. The key to German Pinscher and children is that the puppy must be trained and corrected appropriately. Once the German Pinscher understands how he and the children should interact, he will be very accepting of other children as well as his own.

The German Pinscher can also become protective of his food and things. He needs to understand at an early age that growling and snapping at humans is not acceptable. Household behavior needs to

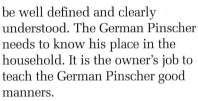

AMONG THE BRIGHTEST OF ALL DOGS
The Pinscher is honored with a mention by one of the most distinguished writers on canine matters, Konrad Lorenz. In his book *Man Meets Dog*, he discusses the relative merits of different breeds and their ancestry. In the chapter titled, "What a pity he can't speak—he understands every word," he reflects upon the canine capacity to understand and the ability of dogs to demonstrate their intelligence and perceptiveness. He gives the Poodle first place for its sagacity but next he places the German Shepherd along with the Pinscher and Giant Schnauzer.

be well defined and clearly understood. The German Pinscher needs to know his place in the household. It is the owner's job to teach the German Pinscher good manners.

True to his heritage, the German Pinscher does not back down from disputes with other dogs. While some German Pinschers can live peacefully with others of the breed of both sexes, it is highly recommended that pairings be of opposite sexes. Be especially careful of other family pets of the small mammal family, including rats, hamsters, guinea pigs and even small toy-breed dogs. While, with time and patience, the German Pinscher can

Ch. Windamir's Tazar Des Charmettes is a clear red.

problem. The most common trait seen when the German Pinscher has developed high anxiety is spinning.

The German Pinscher is not a chronic barker unless he lives with other dogs that do so and he picks up the behavior from other yappy housemates. Above all, remember that the German Pinscher will love you no matter what you do!

COLORS AND COAT

The German Pinscher coat is short, dense and smooth. It should lie close to the body. There are two types of coat that are equally acceptable in the German Pinscher. The softer, shiny coat is most often seen in the US. The harder, coarser coat, which is wiry like a Schnauzer's coat, is also acceptable considering the breed's origins. The harder coat

be taught to accept these other animals, he should never be left with them unsupervised.

The German Pinscher's love of his family can also lead to behavioral problems if not handled carefully. If you baby the German Pinscher puppy, you can very easily create a high-anxiety adult. Constant crating will result in the same

Windamir's Viper Des Charmettes is a mahogany red.

A VERSATILE VICTOR

The Pinscher is one of the most versatile of all dogs. Not only have Pinschers competed with success in all of the usual dog events, but many have become certified as Canine Good Citizens® and also have been part of dog display and road safety teams. In breed competitions, the Pinscher has gained the highest awards at obedience and agility trials and is an exceptional tracker. Pinschers have been trained to be highly successful "hearing dogs" for the deaf and even search and rescue dogs. Properly motivated, there is nothing that the Pinscher cannot tackle or achieve.

Windamir's Sayzar (black with tan markings) with his sire, Ch. LaZar Des Charmettes CD (stag red).

is regularly seen in Europe.

The German Pinscher comes in a wide variety of coat colors. The two categories of colors are self-colored and bi-colored. Self-colored dogs are those that are solid reds and fawns without red/tan markings. The black hairs that are seen in the stag reds are not considered markings, and a stag red German Pinscher is still considered to be self-colored. Bi-colors are the blacks and the blues with tan/red markings.

The most common color is red, which can range from a very light red tone to a dark mahogany. A rich, vibrant red color of a medium to darker shade is preferred. Further, the red color can be a stag red that has black hairs intermingled in the coat. Alternatively, the coat can be a clear red that does not have the black hairs. Both the clear red and the stag red will have the distinctive black "eyeliner" that enhances the expression of the dog. They will also have black noses and lips as well as black nails. In order for breeders to preserve the preferred rich red color, a black with red/tan markings must be bred into the line at least every three generations or the red color will start to pale.

The second most seen color is the black with red/tan markings.

Ch. Icon's Titan Des Charmettes is a stag red. Note the black around the eyes.

This Doberman-like coloration is particularly striking in the German Pinscher. This is why the German Pinscher is often mistaken for a Doberman puppy or small

Windamir's Show Me Blue is a blue with tan markings.

Doberman. The markings should be a rich red/tan in color. The markings, which are the size of a thumb print, appear on the head at the cheeks, lips, lower jaw and above the eyes. Markings on the body are at the throat, below the tail and on the forechest as two distinctly separated triangles. Markings also appear on the legs at the pasterns, forelegs, feet and inner side of the hind legs. Pencil markings on the toes are acceptable. The edges of the markings should be clearly defined as if drawn with a sharp pencil. The bleeding together of the two colors is not acceptable.

The German Pinscher also comes in blue with red/tan markings that are distributed identically to the blacks as described above.

The lightest German Pinscher coat color is the Isabella, which is a fawn color. The fawn can come in several tonal versions including red fawn, black fawn and blue fawn. While the fawns will have the dark nose and lips seen in the other colors, they are the only ones that will consistently have light-colored nails. Blues will occasionally have light-colored nails but not as often as the fawns. Both the fawns and blues have a lighter coat, and the skin coloration can be seen through the coat.

Regardless of the coat color, white markings on the dog are undesirable. A few white hairs do not constitute a marking.

Author Sharon Morgan, who is one of the few people in the United States who has lived with all of the different coat colors, has found that the lighter the coat color, the softer the dog's personality. The blacks have the strongest personality and drive followed by the reds, blues and, finally, the fawns.

TAILS, DEWCLAWS AND EARS
In the US, the tails are docked, the dewclaws are removed and the ears are cropped. While some Americans have chosen to keep the natural ears, the majority still prefer the long, elegant cut similar to that of the Doberman.

German Pinscher breeders and owners in Europe can no longer crop and dock their dogs regardless of their pet or show status. Therefore, dogs imported from these countries will arrive with long tails and natural ears. While the tail can still be docked even on an adult German Pinscher, the dog may be too old to have the long, elegant ear cut done successfully.

The natural German Pinscher ear varies in size but should be triangular in shape. The ear will crease about one quarter of the way down. A few German Pinschers have natural ears that will stand by themselves but most break and point toward the cheek. In addition, the natural-eared German Pinscher will have a number of ear problems that are not seen in the ones that have been cropped. Primarily, because the earflap covers the ear canal, the dog can be more prone to ear infections. In addition, the tip of the ear will sometimes split and bleed, which will leave a notch in the ear leather when healed.

When the puppy is three days old the tail is usually docked between the second and third joint. The length of the tail should match the dog and complement the overall profile of each individual. Most breeders in the US remove front dewclaws at the same time they dock the tail. In all of her years of breeding German Pinschers, the author does not recall seeing a puppy with rear dewclaws.

THE GERMAN PINSCHER'S I.Q.
The German Pinscher is alert, highly intelligent and vivacious. Sometimes they are too smart for their own good. At a very early age, they can out-think the average owner. This high level of intelligence is sometimes referred to as "primitive" or "native" intelligence, which means that the breed is a "thinking breed." Some dogs will obey a command just because it is given even if their unquestioning obedience will result in injury. A thinking breed will not obey a command just because it is given. This is why the German Pinscher needs variety and may become bored with traditional repetitive obedience routines.

HEALTH CONSIDERATIONS
Overall the German Pinscher is a healthy breed with few problems. Many of the early issues have been resolved. These include bad bites and missing teeth, umbilical hernias and demodectic mange.

When bad bites and/or missing teeth do occur in today's German Pinscher, they will usually show up after the baby teeth (deciduous teeth) come out at approximately six months of age. The German Pinscher will usually retain baby eye teeth. It is important that you constantly watch the bite as the adult teeth start to erupt. Retained teeth will have to be removed by a veterinarian unless they are extremely loose.

Umbilical hernias are no longer a physical defect but are usually the result of an overzealous mother, which is why most breeders stay with the female when she is having her litter.

Demodectic mange (demodicosis) occasionally occurs but is usually the result of stress such as air shipping, removal from littermates, being left home alone after returning from a vacation or long-term kenneling. Demodectic mange is sometimes referred to as "teenage mange" and will occur during strong hormonal flows such as a female's first season and a male's first breeding. In the German Pinscher, demodectic mange is usually localized and will resolve itself. Very few German Pinschers of today have generalized demodectic mange that can result in life-long skin problems.

The majority of German Pinscher breeders health-test their breeding stock for hips, eyes and heart. Some breeders also test for the bleeding disorder known as von Willebrand's disease (vWD), but this author has never heard of a case of vWD in a German Pinscher though it is prevalent in Dobermans. Remember that the German Pinscher is more closely related to the Schnauzer and has only acted as one of the ancestral dogs for the Doberman.

A few German Pinschers have exhibited thyroid problems, but these are only occasional and are not common to the breed.

Juvenile cataracts have been seen in some German Pinschers and tend to cluster according to lines. The author has only heard of one instance of progressive retinal atrophy (PRA) in the breed.

Addison's disease is the most serious health problem facing the German Pinscher today. Addison's disease is the common name for hypoadrenocorticism or adrenal insufficiency. It is a disease with symptoms that are common to many other ailments, making diagnosis difficult. The symptoms of Addison's disease can be vague. Initially, the dog may be listless or seem depressed. Many dogs are described as just seeming "off" or losing the normal sparkle in their

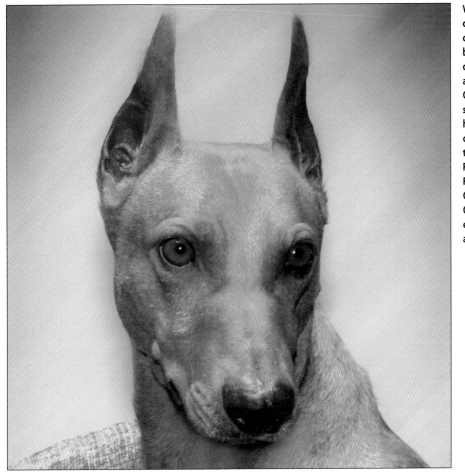

While eye conditions aren't common in the breed, juvenile cataracts have affected some German Pinschers, so it is wise to have your dog certified through the Canine Eye Registration Foundation. This is Ch. LaZar Des Charmettes CD at eleven years of age.

eye. Lack of appetite is a good indicator. Other symptoms include gastrointestinal problems such as vomiting and diarrhea. Pain in the hindquarters or generalized muscle weakness, as indicated by a dog's inability to jump onto the bed or couch as he had done in the past, is not uncommon. Shivering or muscle tremors may also be present. The most important thing to remember is that you know your dog better than anyone else. If something seems amiss, have it checked out. Once Addison's disease is correctly diagnosed, a properly treated dog can live a normal active life.

The oldest German Pinschers on record in the US are a mother and son aged 17 and 19 years, respectively. Today most German Pinscher deaths are a result of cancer.

GERMAN PINSCHER

A breed standard is important as a blueprint for breeders worldwide. A written and agreed-upon statement of requirements should assist in the attempt to produce as perfect a specimen of any particular breed. Although there are minor differences within the various standards, it is still possible to produce a Pinscher that satisfies most of the basic requirements of the breed. In an ideal world all breed standards would indeed be standard, making for ease of importing and exporting dogs with the qualities needed in the breed. Even so, nothing can

An ideal German Pinscher head showing correct type, structure and proportion of a red dog.

stop different breeders, quite legitimately, from making varying interpretations of exactly the same texts and formats.

First we will review the American Kennel Club standard, which is the only standard endorsed by the German Pinscher Club of America and its membership, and then we will present the interim standard of The Kennel Club of England.

THE AKC STANDARD FOR THE GERMAN PINSCHER

GENERAL APPEARANCE

The German Pinscher is a medium size, short-coated dog, elegant in appearance with a strong square build and moderate body structure, muscular and powerful for endurance and agility. Energetic, watchful, alert, agile, fearless, determined, intelligent and loyal, the German Pinscher has the prerequisites to be an excellent watchdog and companion. The German Pinscher is examined on the ground.

SIZE, PROPORTION, SUBSTANCE

Size—the ideal height at the highest point of the withers for a dog or bitch is 17–20 inches. Size should be penalized in accordance with the degree it deviates from the ideal. Quality should always take precedence over size. *Faults*— under 17 inches or over 20 inches. *Proportion*—squarely built in proportion of body length to height. The height at the highest point of the withers equals the length of the body from the prosternum to the rump. *Substance*—muscular with moderate bone.

HEAD AND SKULL

Powerful, elongated without the occiput being too pronounced and resembles a blunt wedge in both frontal and profile views. The total length of the head from the tip of the nose to the occiput is one half the length from the withers to the base of the tail, resulting in a ratio of approximately 1:2. *Expression*— sharp, alert and responsive. *Eyes*— medium size, dark, oval in shape without the appearance of bulging. The eyelid should be tight and the eyeball non-protruding. *Ears*—set high, symmetrical and carried erect when cropped. If uncropped, they are V-shaped with a folding pleat, or small standing ears carried evenly upright. *Skull*—flat, unwrin-kled from occiput to stop when in repose. The stop is slight but distinct. *Muzzle*—parallel and equal in length to the topskull and ends in a blunt wedge. The cheeks are muscled and flat. *Nose*—full,

and black. *Lips*—black, close fitting. *Bite*—strong, scissors bite with complete dentition and white teeth.

NECK, TOPLINE, BODY

Neck—elegant and strong, of moderate thickness and length, nape elegantly arched. The skin is tight, closely fitting to the dry throat without wrinkles, sagging or dewlaps. *Topline*—the withers form the highest point of the topline, which slopes slightly toward the rear, extending in a straight line from behind the withers, through the well-muscled loin to the faintly curved croup. *Back*—short, firm and level, muscular at the loins. *Faults*—long back, not giving the appearance of squarely built, roach back, sway back. *Body*—compact and strong,

Fully mature male, looking sharp and ready for the show ring.

An ideal German Pinscher shown in profile. It has the correct type, structure and proportion.

approximately 90 degree angle to the upper arm, which is equal in length to the shoulder blade. Such angulation permits the maximum forward extension of the forelegs without binding or effort. *Forelegs*—straight and well boned, perfectly vertical when viewed from all sides, set moderately apart so as to permit greater flexibility and agility, with the length of leg being equal to the depth of body. *Loin*—is well muscled. The distance from the last rib to the hip is short. *Chest*—moderately wide with well-sprung ribs, and when viewed from the front, appears to be oval. The forechest is distinctly marked by the prosternum. The brisket descends to the elbows and ascends gradually to the rear with the belly moderately drawn up. *Fault*—excessive tuck up. *Tail*—moderately set and carried above the horizontal. Customarily docked between the second and third joints.

FOREQUARTERS
The sloping shoulder blades are strongly muscled, yet flat and well laid back, forming an angle of approximately 45 degrees to the horizontal. They are well angled and slope forward, forming an

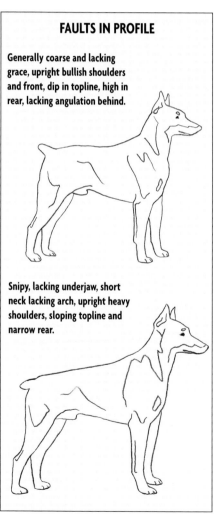

FAULTS IN PROFILE

Generally coarse and lacking grace, upright bullish shoulders and front, dip in topline, high in rear, lacking angulation behind.

Snipy, lacking underjaw, short neck lacking arch, upright heavy shoulders, sloping topline and narrow rear.

with elbows set close to the body. Dewclaws on the forelegs may be removed. *Pasterns*—firm and almost perpendicular to the ground. *Feet*—short, round, compact with firm dark pads and dark nails. The toes are well closed and arched like cat feet.

HINDQUARTERS
The thighs are strongly muscled and in balance with forequarters. The stifles are well bent and well boned, with good angulation. When viewed from the rear, the hocks are parallel to each other.

COAT
Short and dense, smooth and close lying. Shiny and covers the body without bald spots. A hard coat should not be penalized.

COLOR
Isabella (fawn), to red in various shades to stag red (red with intermingling of black hairs), black and blues with red/tan markings. In the reds, a rich vibrant medium to dark shade is preferred. In bi-colored dogs, sharply marked dark and rich red/tan markings are desirable. Markings distributed as follows: at cheeks, lips, lower jaw, above eyes, at throat, on forechest as two triangles distinctly separated from each other, at metatarsus or pasterns, forelegs, feet, inner side of hind legs and below tail. Pencil marks on the toes are acceptable. Any white

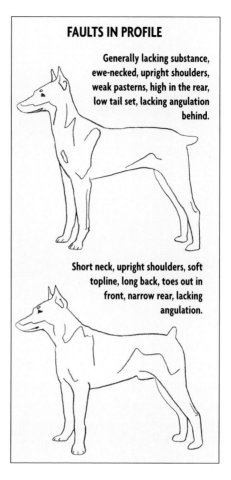

FAULTS IN PROFILE

Generally lacking substance, ewe-necked, upright shoulders, weak pasterns, high in the rear, low tail set, lacking angulation behind.

Short neck, upright shoulders, soft topline, long back, toes out in front, narrow rear, lacking angulation.

markings on the dog are undesirable. A few white hairs do not constitute a marking. *Disqualification*—dogs not of an allowable color.

GAIT
The ground covering trot is relaxed, well balanced, powerful and uninhibited with good length of stride, strong drive and free front extension. At the trot the

Here is an example of a clear red German Pinscher with no eyeliner.

strangers. He has fearless courage and tenacity if threatened. A very vivacious dog, but not an excessive barker. He should not show viciousness by unwarranted or unprovoked attacks. *Note*—great consideration should be given to a dog giving the desired alert, highly intelligent, vivacious character of the German Pinscher. Aggressive behavior towards another dog is not deemed viciousness. *Fault*—shy.

back remains firm and level, without swaying, rolling or roaching. When viewed from the front and rear, the feet must not cross or strike each other. *Fault*—hackney gait.

The foregoing description is that of the ideal German Pinscher. Any deviation from this is to be penalized to the extent of the deviation.

TEMPERAMENT

The German Pinscher has highly developed senses, intelligence, aptitude for training, fearlessness and endurance. He is alert, vigilant, deliberate and watchful of

DISQUALIFICATION

Dogs not of an allowable color.

AUTHOR'S COMMENTS ABOUT THE AKC STANDARD

The German Pinscher goes through a myriad of changes before he reaches maturity between three and four years of age. The head will mature and broaden at about 18 months of age. The topline will go up and down, front and rear as the puppy grows and the adolescent matures. Movement will go from smooth to hackney almost overnight and back again the following week. The chest will usually drop and broaden at about 18 months of age.

The German Pinscher topline is not perfectly level. There is a

In conformation this German Pinscher would be faulted for having a roached back.

slight descent from the highest point of the shoulder to the back, which is strong and muscular. There is then a slight rise over the loin. This is the result of the dog's strong musculature. As the muscle develops over the kidneys, the slight rise develops and affects the topline. Thus, young dogs may not exhibit this trait. Rather, the puppy and adolescent German Pinscher may show a level topline from shoulders to tail or rise and fall in varying degrees as a result of unequal growth spurts.

The current AKC standard states that the tail should be moderately set and carried above the horizontal. While this description is primarily regarding the docked tails that are commonly seen in the US, it has been applied to German Pinschers with undocked tails. The FCI standard describes the undocked tail as "natural" and does not describe the way it should be carried. However, it is the general consensus on the international front that the tail should not curve over the back.

Regarding the coat, bald spots should be penalized but hair loss from scarring that is a result of what is called "honorable wounds" is allowable. Regarding color of the coat, there is no preference in the German Pinscher, and all accepted colors should be treated equally in the show ring. It is true that certain owners, breeders and judges have color preferences and will only keep and/or show certain colors.

The German Pinscher has come a long way from the early days in the US. These early dogs had problems with teeth, round eyes

and extremely splayed feet. Today's German Pinschers are much improved as a result of the efforts of a number of serious breeders who have spent many years selectively breeding their dogs. These problems, such as round eyes which took five generations to breed out, were not easy to correct but are only seen occasionally in the German Pinschers that are being shown.

With the docked tail traditionally seen on dogs in the US, this is Ch. LaZar Des Charmettes CD, winning Best of Opposite Sex in 1997.

INTRODUCTION TO THE ENGLISH STANDARD

By Gloria Cuthbert

The Society for Improving Dog Breeds in Germany produced a series of breed points for the Pinscher in 1880/81. The introduction of these points actually rescued the breed from complete oblivion and gave details on body, tail, color and also conformation faults. It also expressed doubts about whether the Pinscher was first bred in Germany or was only the progeny of the old English Black and Tan Terriers (Manchester Terriers). In an attempt to rid the breed of the terrier influence, the breed points stated that the foreface should be shorter than the English terrier and the skull more rounded and broader. Both cropped and uncropped ears plus docked and undocked tails were permitted.

It was not until 1923 that the original standard was thoroughly reviewed. From then on, only in very extreme cases were smooth-coated dogs registered as Pinschers if they were descended from Schnauzers. The Pinscher breed was to stand alone. The true Pinscher was elegant, well muscled and square with a height of 17–19 inches, and there were a number of approved colors. In 1957 the Pinscher-Schnauzer-Klub issued their first official standard in conjunction with the Fédération Cynologique Internationale (FCI).

The standard noted the Pinscher's anatomical similarity to the Schnauzer, but that the smooth-coated dog should display a more noble appearance. As the faults included small slanting eyes and narrow terrier fronts, it's evident that breeders were concerned about the terrier influence that was still within the breed. In the 1973–1981 FCI standard, the bite is mentioned for the first time and is described as a complete scissors bite. The eye was to be oval, medium in size and dark. Docking of the tails was now universally accepted in the breed, and it was stated that the tail dock should be made after the third joint.

When the Pinscher first came to the UK, there was no real breed standard in existence in the country, but, with recognition of the breed by The Kennel Club, the UK Pinscher Club was asked to produce an interim breed standard, which was approved in July 2001. The current FCI standard was used as the basis for this interim standard. However, there were certain constraints, as it had to be written conforming to The Kennel Club's format. This meant that a section on movement had to be added and because of majority feeling within the breed club then, certain colors were also included. Thus the blue/tan and fawn colors were added as acceptable. There was, at that time, no FCI ruling on uncropped ears apart from set high and dropped. Later, of course, when more European countries ceased cropping, it was noted that a minority, but significant minority, of Pinschers had naturally erect ears. The FCI catered to this natural occurrence and allowed for uncropped ears to be either dropped or symmetrically erect. They also changed the height regulation to allow for dogs of almost 20 inches. The UK interim standard, however, did not change—thus it differs slightly on height allowance, ear carriage and allowed colors from the FCI Pinscher breed standard.

German Pinschers in the UK (called simply Pinschers) and on the Continent are seen with natural ears, V-shaped, folded over and lying close to the head.

THE KENNEL CLUB STANDARD FOR THE PINSCHER (INTERIM)

General Appearance: Well balanced, smooth coated, medium size with elegant and flowing outlines but strong and well muscled.

Characteristics: Alert, good-natured, playful. Loyal, watchful and fearless.

Temperament: High-spirited and self-possessed.

Head and Skull: Seen from above and side resembles a blunt wedge. Strong but not heavy, elongated without pronounced occiput. Overall length in proportion to back (from withers to base of tail) is approximately 1:2. Top of muzzle parallel with extended line of unwrinkled flat forehead; slight but distinct stop. Cheek muscles strong but not prominent. Deep muzzle. Nose full and black; in reds, nose of corresponding shade. Lips tight and dark. Snipiness undesirable.

Eyes: Dark, of medium size, oval and directed forward. Eye rims tight.

Ears: Set high. V-shaped, folded down close to head.

Mouth: Jaws strong with a perfect, regular and complete scissor bite, i.e. upper teeth closely overlapping lower teeth and set square to the jaws.

Neck: Elegant and strong. Neither short nor stout. Nape well arched. Skin of throat tight without dewlap.

Forequarters: Well laid shoulder with good but flat muscle. Forelegs straight viewed from all sides, parallel elbows are close to body.

Body: Chest moderately wide with flat ribs. Brisket extends below elbow. Forechest extends beyond point of shoulder. Compact and short coupled. Length of body approximately equal to height at withers. Back short and slightly sloping. Slightly rounded croup.

Hindquarters: Seen from behind parallel, with sufficient width. Upper thigh slanted and strongly muscled. Good length and bend of stifle, hocks turning neither in nor out.

Feet: Well arched, compact and cat-like with dark nails. Turning neither in nor out. Tough, hard pads.

Tail: Customarily docked. Docked: Docked to three joints. Set and carried high. Undocked: Set and carried high with an upward sweep. In overall balance with the rest of the dog.

Gait/Movement: Free, well balanced and vigorous with good reach in front and strong rotary driving action from rear. Front and hind legs should not be thrown outwards. Topline should remain strong and firm. Hackney movement undesirable.

Coat: Short and dense, smoothly fitting, glossy without bald spots.

Colour: All solid colours from fawn (Isabella) to stag red in various shades. Black and blue with reddish/tan markings. In bi-coloured dogs sharply marked red/tan markings desirable. Markings distributed as follows: at cheeks, lips, lower jaw, above eyes, at throat, at forechest as two triangles separated from each other, at metatarsus, forelegs, feet, inner side of hindlegs and vent region.

Size: Height at withers 43–48 cms (17–19 ins).

Faults: Any departure from the foregoing points should be considered a fault and the seriousness with which the fault should be regarded should be in exact proportion to its degree and its effect upon the health and welfare of the dog.

Note: Male animals should have two apparently normal testicles fully descended into the scrotum.

Despite minor differences, all breed standards for the German Pinscher describe essentially the same medium-sized, well-muscled, alert and courageous dog.

GERMAN PINSCHER

GROWING UP IS HARD TO DO

The German Pinscher will generally reach his full height size by about nine months of age. He will then start to put on body weight and muscle up, but this process could take at least another year. The German Pinscher does remain very puppylike in behavior up until about his second birthday, but from then on one starts to notice (thankfully) definite signs of maturity.

SELECTING A PINSCHER PUPPY

Before you decide to buy a Pinscher puppy, you will need a great deal of thought and discussion with all those involved in his upbringing. This is not the easiest of breeds to own. Try to see adult dogs in a home environment before you make the final decision. Contact one of the breeders recommended by the national parent club, as these dedicated fanciers are the most reliable source for a well-bred puppy. Once you are lucky enough to locate a litter, make sure that you see the dam; often it is possible to see the puppy's sire too. Do not be too hidebound as to which color you prefer, or even which sex. Ask your breeder about any subtle differences. It has been noted by some that the reds tend to mature earlier and the black/tans age more slowly. A myth to be dispelled is that if the tan triangles in the black/tan puppies are not properly divided, they never will be. Most dogs with little or no division at birth have two perfectly formed

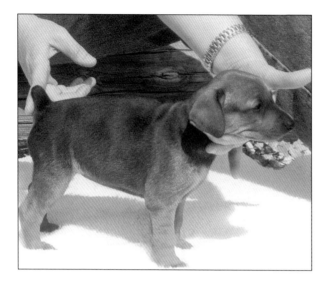

Pinscher adults are meant to be wary but that puppies usually respond well to human attention.

A COMMITTED NEW OWNER

By now you should understand what makes the German Pinscher a most unique and special dog, one that may fit nicely into your family and lifestyle. If you have researched breeders, you should be able to recognize a knowledgeable and responsible German Pinscher breeder who cares not only about his pups but also about what kind of owner you will be. If you have completed the final step in your new journey, you have found a litter, or possibly two, of quality German Pinscher pups.

A visit with the puppies and their breeder should be an education in itself. Breed research, breeder selection and puppy visitation are very important aspects of finding the puppy of your dreams. Beyond that, these things also lay the foundation for a successful future with your pup. Puppy personalities within each litter vary, from the shy and easygoing puppy to the one who is dominant and assertive, with most pups falling somewhere in between. By spending time with the puppies you will be able to

The breeder will likely want to assess the show potential of his litter before deciding which pups to part with and which ones to keep for future showing and/or breeding.

tan triangles by maturity. Similarly, some straw or dark streaks in the red puppies can lighten or disappear to the desired clear red coloration. However, light pigmentation of the nails, nose and eye very rarely darkens with age.

Look for a happy, healthy puppy, having noted the dam's temperament. Remember that

A well-tempered pup won't mind being handled by visitors to the kennel; if he does, this is a red flag that this dog may become quite a handful.

recognize certain behaviors and what these behaviors indicate about each pup's temperament. Which type of pup will complement your family dynamics is best determined by observing the puppies in action within their "pack." Your breeder's expertise and recommendations are also valuable. Although you may fall in love with a bold and brassy male, the breeder may suggest that another pup would be best for you. The breeder's experience in rearing German Pinscher pups and matching their temperaments with appropriate humans offers the best assurance that your pup will meet your needs and expectations. The type of puppy that you select is just as important as your decision that the German Pinscher is the breed for you.

The decision to live with a German Pinscher is a serious

BETTER THAN THE AVERAGE DOG

Even though you may never show your dog, you should still read the breed standard. The breed standard tells you more than just physical specifications such as how tall your dog should be; it also describes how he should act, how he should move and what unique qualities make him the breed that he is. You are not investing money in a pure-bred dog so that you can own a dog that "sort of looks like" the breed you're purchasing. You want a typical, handsome representative of the breed, one that all of your friends and family and people you meet out in public will recognize as the breed you've so carefully selected and researched. If the parents of your prospective puppy bear little or no resemblance to the dog described in the breed standard, you should keep searching!

This German Pinscher's ears are freshly cropped and braced.

commitment and not one to be taken lightly. This puppy is a living sentient being that will be dependent on you for basic survival for his entire life. Beyond the basics of survival—food, water, shelter and protection—he needs much, much more. The new pup needs love, nurturing and a proper canine education to mold him into a responsible, well-behaved canine citizen. Your German Pinscher's health and good manners will need consistent monitoring and regular "tune-ups," so your job as a responsible dog owner will be ongoing throughout every stage of his life. The German Pinscher is a long-lived breed, and you must be prepared to accept these responsi-

Starting with a well-bred, sound and healthy puppy will give you an alert, versatile and long-lived adult with proper care.

SOME DAM ATTITUDE

When selecting a puppy, be certain to meet the dam of the litter. The temperament of the dam is often predictive of the temperament of her puppies. However, dams occasionally are very protective of their young, some to the point of being testy or aggressive with visitors, whom they may view as a danger to their babies. Such attitudes are more common when the pups are very young and still nursing and should not be mistaken for actual aggressive temperament. If possible, visit the dam away from her pups to make friends with her and gain a better understanding of her true personality.

bilities and commit to them for the entire lifetime of the dog. Although the responsibilities of owning a dog may at times tax your patience, the joy of living with your German Pinscher far outweighs the workload, and a well-mannered adult dog is worth your time and effort. Before your very eyes, your new charge will grow up to be your most loyal friend.

YOUR GERMAN PINSCHER SHOPPING LIST

Just as expectant parents prepare a nursery for their baby, so should you ready your home for the arrival of your German Pinscher pup. If you have the necessary puppy supplies purchased and in place before he comes home, it will ease the puppy's transition from the warmth and familiarity of his mom and littermates to the brand-new environment of his new home and human family. You will be too busy to stock up and prepare your house after your pup comes home, that's for sure! Imagine how a pup must feel upon being transported to a strange new place. It's up to you to comfort him and to let your little pup know that he is going to be happy with you.

FOOD AND WATER BOWLS

Your puppy will need separate bowls for his food and water. Stainless steel pans are generally preferred over plastic bowls since they sterilize better and pups are less inclined to chew on the metal. Heavy-duty ceramic bowls are popular, but consider how often you will have to pick up those heavy bowls. Buy adult-sized pans, as your puppy will grow into them before you know it.

THE DOG CRATE

If you think that crates are tools of punishment and confinement for when a dog has misbehaved, think again. Most breeders and almost all trainers recommend a crate as the preferred house-training aid as well as for all-around puppy training and safety. Because dogs are natural den creatures that

prefer cave-like environments, the benefits of crate use are many. The crate provides the puppy with his very own "safe house," a cozy place to sleep, take a break or seek comfort with a favorite toy; a travel aid to house your dog when on the road, at motels or at the vet's office; a training aid to help teach your puppy proper toileting habits; and a place of solitude

CRATE EXPECTATIONS

To make the crate more inviting to your puppy, you can offer his first meal or two inside the crate, always keeping the crate door open so that he does not feel confined. Keep a favorite toy or two in the crate for him to play with while inside. You can also cover the crate at night with a lightweight sheet to make it more den-like and remove the stimuli of household activity. Never put him into his crate as punishment or as you are scolding him, since he will then associate his crate with negative situations and avoid going there.

WHAT SIZE IS THE RIGHT SIZE?

When purchasing a crate, buy one that will fit an adult-size dog. Puppy crates are poor investments, since puppies quickly outgrow them. The crate should accommodate an adult dog in a standing position so that he has room to stand up, turn around and lie down comfortably. A larger crate is fine but not necessary for the dog's comfort, as most of his crate time will be spent lying down and napping.

most popular. Both are safe and your puppy will adjust to either one, so the choice is up to you. The wire crates offer better visibility for the pup as well as better ventilation. Many of the wire crates easily collapse into suitcase-size carriers. The fiberglass crates, similar to those used by the airlines for animal transport, are sturdier and more den-like. However, the fiberglass crates do not collapse and are less ventilated than wire crates; this can be problematic in hot weather. Some of the newer crates are made of heavy plastic mesh; they are very lightweight and fold up into slim-line suitcases. However, a mesh crate might not be suitable for a pup with manic chewing habits.

Don't bother with a puppy-sized crate. Although your German Pinscher will be a wee fellow when you bring him home, he will grow up in the blink of an eye and your puppy crate will be useless. Purchase a crate that will accommodate an adult German Pinscher. He will stand about 17 to 20 inches when full grown, so a medium- to large-sized crate will fit him nicely.

BEDDING AND CRATE PADS

Your puppy will enjoy some type of soft bedding in his "room" (the crate), something he can snuggle into to feel cozy and secure. Old towels or blankets are good choices

when non-dog people happen to drop by and don't want a lively puppy—or even a well-behaved adult dog—saying hello or begging for attention.

Crates come in several types, although the wire crate and the fiberglass airline-type crate are the

for a young pup, since he may (and probably will) have a toileting accident or two in the crate or decide to chew on the bedding material. Once he is fully trained and out of the early chewing stage, you can replace the puppy bedding with a permanent crate pad if you prefer. Crate pads and other dog beds run the gamut from inexpensive to high-end doggie-designer styles, but don't splurge on the good stuff until you are sure that your puppy is reliable and won't tear it up or make a mess on it.

PUPPY TOYS

Just as infants and older children require objects to stimulate their minds and bodies, puppies need toys to entertain their curious brains, wiggly paws and achy teeth. A fun array of safe doggie toys will help satisfy your puppy's chewing instincts and distract him from gnawing on the leg of your antique chair or your new leather

TOYS 'R SAFE

The vast array of tantalizing puppy toys is staggering. Stroll through any pet shop or pet-supply outlet and you will see that the choices can be overwhelming. However, not all dog toys are safe or sensible. Most very young puppies enjoy soft woolly toys that they can snuggle with and carry around. (You know they have outgrown them when they shred them up!) Avoid toys that have buttons, tabs or other enhancements that can be chewed off and swallowed. Soft toys that squeak are fun, but make sure your puppy does not disembowel the toy and remove (and swallow) the squeaker. Toys that rattle or make noise can excite a puppy, but they present the same danger as the squeaky kind and so require supervision. Hard rubber toys that bounce can also entertain a pup, but make sure that the toy is too big for your pup to swallow.

A sleepy German Pinscher will welcome a cozy place to rest. Invest in a good-quality bed that is large enough to accommodate a fully grown dog.

COLLARING OUR CANINES

The standard flat collar with a buckle or a snap, in leather, nylon or cotton, is widely regarded as the everyday all-purpose collar. If the collar fits correctly, you should be able to fit two fingers between the collar and the dog's neck.

Leather Buckle Collars

Limited-Slip Collar

Snap-Bolt Choke Collar

The martingale, Greyhound or limited-slip collar is preferred by many dog owners and trainers. It is fixed with an extra loop that tightens when pressure is applied to the leash. The martingale collar gets tighter but does not "choke" the dog. The limited-slip collar should only be used for walking and training, not for free play or interaction with another dog. These types of collar should never be left on the dog, as the extra loop can lead to accidents.

Choke collars, usually made of stainless steel, are made for training purposes but are not recommended for small dogs or heavily coated breeds. The chains can injure small dogs or damage long/abundant coats. Thin nylon choke leads are commonly used on show dogs while in the ring, though they are not practical for everyday use.

The harness, with two or three straps that attach over the dog's shoulders and around his torso, is a humane and safe alternative to the conventional collar. By and large, a well-made harness is virtually escape-proof. Harnesses are available in nylon and mesh and can be outfitted on most dogs, with chest girths ranging from 10 to 30 inches.

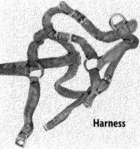

Harness

Nylon Collar

Quick-Click Closure

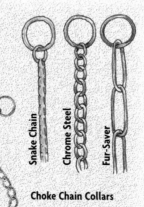

Snake Chain

Chrome Steel

Fur-Saver

Choke Chain Collars

A head collar, composed of a nylon strap that goes around the dog's muzzle and a second strap that wraps around his neck, offers the owner better control over his dog. This device is recommended for problem-solving with dogs (including jumping up, pulling and aggressive behaviors), but must be used with care.

A training halter, including a flat collar and two straps, made of nylon and webbing, is designed for walking. There are several on the market; some are more difficult to put on the dog than others. The halter harness, with two small slip rings at each end, is recommended for ease of use.

sofa. Most puppy toys are cute and look as if they would be a lot of fun, but not all are necessarily safe or good for your puppy, so use caution when you go puppy-toy shopping.

Like many other dogs, German Pinschers enjoy chewing, especially as puppies or when bored. The best "chewcifiers" are nylon and hard rubber bones, which are safe to gnaw on and come in sizes appropriate for all age groups and breeds. Be especially careful of natural bones, which can splinter or develop dangerous sharp edges; pups can easily swallow or choke on those bone splinters. Veterinarians often tell of surgical nightmares involving bits of splintered bone, because in addition to the danger of choking, the sharp pieces can damage the intestinal tract.

Similarly, rawhide chews, while a favorite of most dogs and puppies, can be equally dangerous. Pieces of rawhide are easily swallowed after they get soft and gummy from chewing, and dogs have been known to choke on pieces of ingested rawhide. Rawhide chews should be offered only when you can supervise the puppy.

Soft woolly toys are special puppy favorites. They come in a wide variety of cute shapes and sizes; some look like little stuffed animals. Puppies love to shake them up and toss them about, or

simply carry them around. Be careful, as German Pinscher pups love to de-stuff and de-squeak their toys, and also be careful of fuzzy toys that have button eyes or noses that your pup could chew off and swallow. Braided rope toys are similar in that they are fun to chew and toss around, but they shred easily and the strings are easy to swallow. The strings are not digestible and, if the puppy doesn't pass them in his stool, he could end up at the vet's office. As with rawhides,

These pups are having a ball! Make sure the toys you provide your pups with are ones that won't endanger them.

A dog that loves to chew won't hesitate to chew on her leash—or anything else she isn't supposed to if she isn't provide with safe chew toys.

KEEP OUT OF REACH

Most dogs don't browse around your medicine cabinet, but accidents do happen! The drug acetaminophen, the active ingredient in some pain relievers, can be deadly to dogs and cats if ingested in large quantities. Acetaminophen toxicity, caused by the dog's swallowing 15 to 20 tablets, can be manifested in abdominal pains within a day or two of ingestion, as well as liver damage. If you suspect your dog has swiped a bottle of medicine, get the dog to the vet immediately so that the vet can induce vomiting and cleanse the dog's stomach.

your puppy should be closely monitored with rope toys.

If you believe that your pup has ingested a piece of one of his toys, check his stools for the next couple of days to see if he passes the item when he defecates. At the same time, also watch for signs of intestinal distress. A call to your veterinarian might be in order to get his advice and be on the safe side.

An all-time favorite toy for puppies (young and old!) is the empty gallon milk jug. Hard plastic juice containers—46 ounces or more—are also excellent. Such containers make lots of noise when they are batted about, and puppies go

crazy with delight as they play with them. However, they don't often last very long, so be sure to remove and replace them when they get chewed up on the ends.

A word of caution about homemade toys: be careful with your choices of non-traditional play objects. Never use old shoes or socks, since a puppy cannot distinguish between the old ones on which he's allowed to chew and the new ones in your closet that are strictly off limits. That principle applies to anything that resembles something that you don't want your puppy to chew.

COLLARS

A lightweight nylon collar is the best choice for a very young pup. Quick-click collars are easy to put on and remove, and they can be adjusted as the puppy grows. Introduce him to his collar as soon as he comes home to get him accustomed to wearing it. He'll get used to it quickly and won't mind a bit. Make sure that it is snug enough that it won't slip off, yet loose enough to be comfortable for the pup. You should be able to slip two fingers between the collar and his neck. Check the collar often, as puppies grow in spurts, and his collar can become too tight almost overnight. A choke collar may be needed later for training purposes only, but should never be used on a young puppy.

LEASH LIFE

Dogs love leashes! Believe it or not, most dogs dance for joy every time their owners pick up their leashes. The leash means that the dog is going for a walk—and there are few things more exciting than that! Here are some of the kinds of leashes that are commercially available.

Nylon Leash

Leather Leash

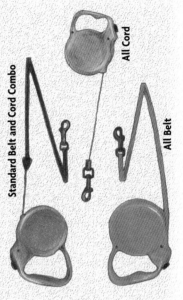

Standard Belt and Cord Combo

All Cord

All Belt

Retractable Leashes

Traditional Leash: Made of cotton, nylon or leather, these leashes are usually about 6 feet in length. A quality-made leather leash is softer on the hands than a nylon one. Durable woven cotton is a popular option. Lengths can vary up to about 48 feet, designed for different uses.

Chain Leash: Usually a metal chain leash with a plastic handle. This is not the best choice for most breeds, as it is heavier than other leashes and difficult to manage.

Retractable Leash: A long nylon cord is housed in a plastic device for extending and retracting. This leash, also known as a flexible leash, is ideal for taking trained dogs for long walks in open areas, although it is not always suitable for large, powerful breeds. Different lengths and sizes are available, so check that you purchase one appropriate for your dog's weight.

Elastic Leash: A nylon leash with an elastic extension. This is useful for well-trained dogs, especially in conjunction with a head halter.

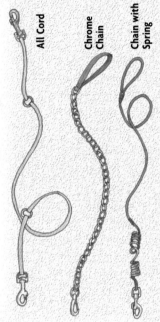

All Cord

Chrome Chain

Chain with Spring

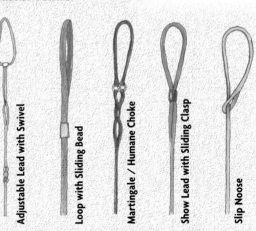

Adjustable Lead with Swivel

Loop with Sliding Bead

Martingale / Humane Choke

Show Lead with Sliding Clasp

Slip Noose

A Variety of Collar-Leash-in-One Products

Avoid leashes that are completely elastic, as they afford minimal control to the handler.

Adjustable Leash: This has two snaps, one on each end, and several metal rings. It is handy if you need to tether your dog temporarily, but is never to be used with a choke collar.

Tab Leash: A short leash (4 to 6 inches long) that attaches to your dog's collar. This device serves like a handle, in case you have to grab your dog while he's exercising off lead. It's ideal for "half-trained" dogs or dogs that listen only half of the time.

Slip Leash: Essentially a leash with a collar built in, similar to what a dog-show handler uses to show a dog. This British-style collar has a ring on the end so that you can form a slip collar. Useful if you have to catch your own runaway dog or a stray.

A Dog-Safe Home

The dog-safety police are taking you and your new puppy on a house tour. Let's go room by room and see how safe your own home is for your new pup. The following items are doggy dangers, so either they must be removed or the dog should be monitored or not allowed access to these areas.

Living Room

- house plants (some varieties are poisonous)
- fireplace or wood-burning stove
- paint on the walls (lead-based paint is toxic)
- lead drapery weights (toxic lead)
- lamps and electrical cords
- carpet cleaners or deodorizers

Outdoors

- swimming pool
- pesticides
- toxic plants
- lawn fertilizers

Bathroom

- blue water in the toilet bowl
- medicine cabinet (filled with potentially deadly bottles)
- soap bars, bleach, drain cleaners, etc.
- tampons

Kitchen

- household cleaners in the kitchen cabinets
- glass jars and canisters
- sharp objects (like kitchen knives, scissors and forks)
- garbage can (with remnants of good-smelling things like onions, potato skins, apple or pear cores, peach pits, coffee beans and other harmful tidbits)
- food left out on counters (some foods are toxic to dogs)

Garage

- antifreeze
- fertilizers (including rose foods)
- pesticides and rodenticides
- pool supplies (chlorine and other chemicals)
- oil and gasoline in containers
- sharp objects, electrical cords and power tools

LEASHES

A 6-foot nylon lead is an excellent choice for a young puppy. It is lightweight and not as tempting to chew as a leather lead. You can switch to a 6-foot leather lead after your pup has grown and is used to walking politely on a lead. For initial puppy walks and house-training purposes, you should invest in a shorter lead so that you have more control over the puppy. At first, you don't want him wandering too far away from you, and when taking him out for toileting you will want to keep him in the specific area chosen for his potty spot.

Once the puppy is heel-trained with a traditional leash, you can consider purchasing a retractable lead. A retractable lead is excellent for walking adult dogs that are already leash-wise. This type of lead allows the dog to roam farther away from you and explore a wider area when out walking, and also retracts when you need to keep him close to you.

HOME SAFETY FOR YOUR PUPPY

The importance of puppy-proofing cannot be overstated. In addition to making your house comfortable for your German Pinscher's arrival, you also must make sure that your house is safe for your puppy before you bring him home. There are countless hazards in the owner's personal living environment that a

Some flowers and plants are toxic and can be harmful if consumed by your German Pinscher. It is important that you puppy-proof your entire home, inside and out.

pup can sniff, chew, swallow or destroy. Many are obvious; others are not. Do a thorough advance house check to remove or rearrange those things that could hurt your puppy, keeping any potentially dangerous items out of areas to which he will have access.

Electrical cords are especially dangerous, since puppies view them as irresistible chew toys. Unplug and remove all exposed cords or fasten them beneath baseboards where the puppy cannot reach them. Veterinarians and firefighters can tell you horror stories about electrical burns and house fires that resulted from puppy-chewed electrical cords. Consider this a most serious

The German Pinscher is very intent when something attracts his interest. A well-fenced yard is necessary so he doesn't get himself into trouble or danger.

precaution for your puppy and the rest of your family.

Scout your home for tiny objects that might be seen at a pup's eye level. Keep medication bottles and cleaning supplies well out of reach, and do the same with waste baskets and other trash containers. It goes without saying that you should not use rodent poison or other toxic chemicals in any puppy area and that you must keep such containers safely locked up. You will be amazed at how many places a curious puppy can discover!

Once your house has cleared inspection, check your yard. A sturdy fence, well embedded into the ground, will give your dog a safe place to play and potty. German Pinschers are athletic dogs, so at least a 6-foot-high fence will be necessary to contain an agile youngster or adult. Check the fence periodically for necessary repairs. If there is a weak link or space to squeeze through, you can be sure a determined German Pinscher will discover it.

The garage and shed can be hazardous places for a pup, as things like fertilizers, chemicals and tools are usually kept there. It's best to keep these areas off limits to the pup. Antifreeze is especially dangerous to dogs, as they find the taste appealing and it takes only a few licks from the driveway to kill a dog, puppy or adult, small breed or large.

ARE VACCINATIONS NECESSARY?

Vaccinations are recommended for all puppies by the American Veterinary Medical Association (AVMA). Some vaccines are absolutely necessary, while others depend upon a dog's or puppy's individual exposure to certain diseases or the animal's immune history. Rabies vaccinations are required by law in all 50 states. Some diseases are fatal whereas others are treatable, making the need for vaccinating against the latter questionable. Follow your veterinarian's recommendations to keep your dog fully immunized and protected. You can also review the AVMA directive on vaccinations on their website: www.avma.org.

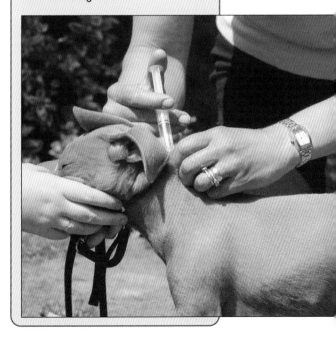

VISITING THE VETERINARIAN

A good veterinarian is your German Pinscher puppy's best health insurance policy. If you do not already have a vet, ask friends and experienced dog people in your area for recommendations so that you can select a vet before you bring your German Pinscher puppy home. Also arrange for your puppy's first veterinary examination well in advance, since many vets have waiting periods and your puppy should visit the vet within a day or so of coming home.

It's important to make sure your puppy's first visit to the vet is a pleasant and positive one. The vet should take great care to befriend the pup and handle him gently to make their first meeting a positive experience. The vet will give the pup a thorough physical examination and set up a schedule for vaccinations and other necessary wellness visits. Be sure to show your vet any health and inoculation records, which

Ch. Windamir's Sahara B as a puppy. German Pinschers love balls of all types.

PEDIGREE VS. REGISTRATION CERTIFICATE

Too often new owners are confused between these two important documents. Your puppy's pedigree, essentially a family tree, is a written record of a dog's genealogy of three generations or more. The pedigree will show you the names as well as performance titles of all dogs in your pup's background. Your breeder must provide you with a registration application, with his part properly filled out. You must complete the application and send it to the AKC with the proper fee. Every puppy must come from a litter that has been AKC-registered by the breeder, born in the US and from a sire and dam that are also registered with the AKC.

The seller must provide you with complete records to identify the puppy. The AKC requires that the seller provide the buyer with the following: breed; sex, color and markings; date of birth; litter number (when available); names and registration numbers of the parents; breeder's name; and date sold or delivered.

you should have received from your breeder. Your vet is a great source of canine health information, so be sure to ask questions and take notes. Creating a health journal for your puppy will make a handy reference for his wellness and any future health problems that may arise.

MEETING THE FAMILY

Your German Pinscher's homecoming is an exciting time for all members of the family, and it's only natural that everyone will be eager to meet him, pet him and play with him. However, for the puppy's sake, it's best to make these initial family meetings as uneventful as possible so that the pup is not overwhelmed with too much too soon. Remember, he has just left his dam and his littermates and is away from the breeder's home for the first time. Despite his little wagging tail, he is still apprehensive and wondering where he is and who all these strange humans are. It's best to let him explore on his own and meet the family members as he feels comfortable. Let him investigate all the new smells, sights and sounds at his own pace. Children should be especially careful to not get overly excited, use loud voices or hug the pup too tightly. Be calm, gentle and affectionate, and be ready to comfort him if he appears

frightened or uneasy.

Be sure to show your puppy his new crate during this first day home. Toss a treat or two inside the crate; if he associates the crate with food, he will associate the crate with good things. If he is comfortable with the crate, you can offer him his first meal inside it. Leave the door ajar so he can wander in and out as he chooses.

Growing up together, children and dogs are likely to form a friendship second to none.

FIRST NIGHT IN HIS NEW HOME

So much has happened in your German Pinscher puppy's first day away from the breeder. He's had his first car ride to his new home. He's met his new human family and perhaps the other family pets. He has explored his new house and yard, at least those places where he is to be allowed during his first weeks at home. He may have visited his new veterinarian. He has eaten his first meal or two away from his dam and littermates. Surely that's enough to tire out an eight-week-old German Pinscher

THE FIRST FAMILY MEETING

Your puppy's first day at home should be quiet and uneventful. Despite his wagging tail, he is still wondering where his mom and siblings are! Let him make friends with other members of the family on his own terms; don't overwhelm him. You have a lifetime ahead to get to know each other!

German Pinschers thrive on being part of the family.

pup—or so you hope!

It's bedtime. During the day, the pup investigated his crate, which is his new den and sleeping space, so it is not entirely strange to him. Line the crate with a soft towel or blanket that he can snuggle into and gently place him into the crate for the night. Some breeders send home a piece of bedding from where the pup slept with his littermates, and those familiar scents are a great comfort for the puppy on his first night without his siblings.

He will probably whine or cry. The puppy is objecting to the confinement and the fact that he is alone for the first time. This can be a stressful time for you as well as for the pup. It's important that you remain strong and don't let the puppy out of his crate to comfort him. He will fall asleep eventually. If you release him, the puppy will learn that crying means "out" and will continue that habit. You are laying the groundwork for future habits. Some breeders find that soft music can soothe a crying pup and help him get to sleep.

SOCIALIZING YOUR PUPPY

The first 20 weeks of your German Pinscher puppy's life are the most important of his entire lifetime. A properly socialized puppy will grow up to be a confident and stable adult who will be a pleasure to live with and a welcome addition to the neighborhood.

The importance of socialization cannot be overemphasized. Research on canine behavior has proven that puppies who are not exposed to new sights, sounds, people and animals during their first 20 weeks of life will grow up to be timid and fearful, even aggressive, and unable to flourish outside of their home environment.

Socializing your puppy is not difficult and, in fact, will be a fun time for you both. Lead training goes hand in hand with socialization, so your puppy will be learning how to walk on a lead at the same time that he's meeting the neighborhood. Because the German Pinscher is such a remarkable breed, your puppy will enjoy being "the new kid on the block." Take him for short walks to the park and to other dog-friendly places where he will encounter new people, especially children. Puppies automatically recognize children as "little people" and are drawn to play with them. Just make sure that

THE GRASS IS ALWAYS GREENER

Must dog owners decide between their beloved canine pals and their perfectly manicured emerald-green lawns? Just as dog urine is no tonic for growing grass, lawn chemicals are extremely dangerous to your dog. Fertilizers, pesticides and herbicides pose real threats to canines and humans alike. Dogs should be kept off treated grounds for at least 24 hours following treatment. Consider some organic options for your lawn care, such as using a homemade compost or a natural fertilizer instead of a commercial chemical. Some dog-conscious lawnkeepers avoid fertilizers

entirely, keeping up their lawns by watering, aerating, mowing and seeding frequently.

As always, dogs complicate the equation. Canines love grass. They roll in it, eat it and love to bury their noses in it—and then do their business in it! Grass can mean hours of feel-good, smell-good fun! In addition to the dangers of lawn-care chemicals, there's also the threat of burs, thorns and pebbles in the grass, not to mention the very common grass allergy. Many dogs develop an incurably itchy skin condition from grass, especially in the late summer when the world is in full bloom.

"fear period." This is a serious imprinting period, and all contact during this time should be gentle and positive. A frightening or negative event could leave a permanent impression that could affect his future behavior if a similar situation arises.

Also make sure that your puppy has received his first and second rounds of vaccinations before you expose him to other dogs or bring him to places that other dogs may frequent. Avoid dog parks and other strange-dog areas until your vet assures you that your puppy is fully immunized and resistant to the diseases that can be passed between canines. Discuss safe socialization with your breeder, as some breeders recommend social-izing the puppy even before he has received all of his inoculations, depending on how outgoing the puppy may be.

Proper socialization is a must if you want your dog to be well-tempered. The naturally curious German Pinscher will love meeting new people.

you supervise these meetings and that the children do not get too rough or encourage him to play too hard. An overzealous pup can often nip too hard, frightening the child and in turn making the puppy overly excited. A bad experience in puppyhood can impact a dog for life, so a pup that has a negative experience with a child may grow up to be shy or even aggressive around children.

Take your puppy along on your daily errands. Puppies are natural "people magnets," and most people who see your pup will want to pet him. All of these encounters will help to mold him into a confident adult dog. Likewise, you will soon feel like a confident, responsible dog owner, rightly proud of your mannerly German Pinscher.

Be especially careful of your puppy's encounters and experi-ences during the eight-to-ten-week-old period, which is also called the

LEADER OF THE PUPPY'S PACK
Like other canines, your puppy needs an authority figure, someone he can look up to and regard as the leader of his "pack." His first pack leader was his dam, who taught him to be polite and not chew too hard on her ears or nip at her muzzle. He learned those same lessons from his littermates. If he played too rough, they cried in pain and stopped the game, which sent an important message to the rowdy puppy.

As puppies play together, they are also struggling to determine who will be the boss. Being pack animals, dogs need someone to be in charge. If a litter of puppies remained together beyond puppyhood, one of the pups would emerge as the strongest one, the one who calls the shots.

Once your puppy leaves the pack, he will look intuitively for a new leader. If he does not recognize you as that leader, he will try to assume that position for himself. Of course, it is hard to imagine your adorable German Pinscher puppy trying to be in charge when he is so small and seemingly helpless. You must remember that these are natural canine instincts. Do not cave in and allow your pup to get the upper "paw"!

Just as socialization is so important during these first 20 weeks, so too is your puppy's early education. He was born without any bad habits. He does not know what is good or bad behavior. If he does things like nipping and digging, it's because he is having fun and doesn't know that humans consider these things as "bad." It's your job to teach him proper puppy manners, and this is the best time to accomplish that—before he has developed bad habits, since it is much more difficult to "unlearn" or correct unacceptable learned behavior than to teach good behavior from the start.

Make sure that all members of the family understand the importance of being consistent when training their new puppy. If you tell the puppy to stay off the sofa and your daughter allows him to cuddle on the couch to watch her favorite television show, your pup will be confused about what he is and is not allowed to do. Have a family conference before

CONFINEMENT

It is wise to keep your puppy confined to a small "puppy-proofed" area of the house initially. Gate or block off a space near the door he will use for outdoor potty trips. If he is allowed to roam through the entire house or even only several rooms, it will be more difficult to house-train him. To let him out off-leash to relieve himself, you must have an escape-proof yard.

Socialization includes introducing your puppy to other pups and adult dogs, always under your watchful eye.

your pup comes home so that everyone understands the basic principles of puppy training and the rules you have set forth for the pup and agrees to follow them.

The old saying that "an ounce of prevention is worth a pound of cure" is especially true when it comes to puppies. It is much easier to prevent inappropriate behavior than it is to change it. It's also easier and less stressful for the pup, since it will keep discipline to a minimum and create a more positive learning environment for him. That, in turn, will also be easier on you.

Here are a few commonsense tips to keep your belongings safe and your puppy out of trouble:

• Keep your closet doors closed and your shoes, socks and other apparel off the floor so your puppy can't get to them.

• Keep a secure lid on the trash container or put the trash where your puppy can't dig into it. He can't damage what he can't reach!

• Supervise your puppy at all times to make sure he is not getting into mischief. If he starts to chew the corner of the rug, you can distract him instantly by tossing a toy for him to fetch. You also will be able to whisk him outside when you notice that he is about to piddle on the carpet. If you can't see your puppy, you can't teach him or correct his behavior.

SOLVING PUPPY PROBLEMS

CHEWING AND NIPPING
Nipping at fingers and toes is normal puppy behavior. Chewing is also the way that puppies

investigate their surroundings. However, you will have to teach your puppy that chewing anything other than his toys is not acceptable. That won't happen overnight and at times puppy teeth will test your patience. However, if you allow nipping and chewing to continue, just think about the damage that a mature German Pinscher can do with a full set of adult teeth.

Whenever your puppy nips your hand or fingers, cry out "Ouch!" in a loud voice, which should startle your puppy and stop him from nipping, even if only for a moment. Immediately distract him by offering a small treat or an appropriate toy for him to chew instead (which means having chew toys and puppy treats handy or in your pockets at all times). Praise him when he takes the toy, and tell him what a good fellow he is. Praise is just as or even more important in puppy training as discipline and correction.

Puppies also tend to nip at children more often than adults, since they perceive little ones to be more vulnerable and more similar to their littermates. Teach your children appropriate responses to nipping behavior. If they are unable to handle it themselves, you may have to intervene. Puppy nips can be quite painful and a child's frightened reaction will only encourage a puppy to nip harder, which is a natural canine response.

As with all other puppy situations, interaction between your German Pinscher puppy and children should be supervised.

BE CONSISTENT
Consistency is absolutely necessary to a puppy's learning environment, whether teaching commands or enforcing the house rules. A behavior (such as chewing, jumping up or climbing onto the furniture) cannot be forbidden one day and then allowed the next. That will only confuse the pup, and he will not understand what he is supposed to do. Just one or two episodes of allowing an undesirable behavior to "slide" will imprint that behavior on a puppy's brain and make that behavior more difficult to erase or change.

Chewing on objects, not just family members' fingers and ankles, is also normal canine behavior that can be especially tedious (for the owner, not the pup) during the teething period when the puppy's adult teeth are coming in. At this stage, chewing just plain feels good. Furniture legs and cabinet corners are common puppy favorites. Shoes and other personal items also taste pretty good to a pup.

The best solution is, once again, prevention. If you value something, keep it tucked away and out of reach. You can't hide your dining-room table in a closet, but you can try to deflect the chewing by applying a bitter product made just to deter dogs from chewing. This spray-on substance is vile-tasting, although safe for dogs, and most puppies will avoid the forbidden object after one tiny taste. You also can apply the product to your leather leash if the puppy tries to chew on his lead during leash-training sessions.

Keep a ready supply of safe chews handy to offer your German Pinscher as a distraction when he starts to chew on something that's a "no-no." Remember, at this tender age he does not yet know what is permitted or forbidden, so you have to be "on call" every minute he's awake and on the prowl.

You may lose a treasure or two during your puppy's growing-up period, and the furniture could sustain a nasty nick or two. These can be trying times, so be prepared for those inevitable accidents and comfort yourself in knowing that this too shall pass.

TEETHING TIME

All puppies chew. It's normal canine behavior. Chewing just plain feels good to a puppy, especially during the three-to five-month teething period when the adult teeth are breaking through the gums. Rather than attempting to eliminate such a strong natural chewing instinct, you will be more successful if you redirect it and teach your puppy what he may or may not chew. Correct inappropriate chewing with a sharp "No!" and offer him a chew toy, praising him when he takes it. Don't become discouraged. Chewing usually decreases after the adult teeth have come in.

JUMPING UP

Although German Pinscher pups are not known to be notorious jumpers, they are still puppies after all, and puppies jump up—on you, your guests, your counters and your furniture. Just another normal part of growing up, and one you need to meet head-on before it becomes an ingrained habit.

The key to jump correction is consistency. You cannot correct your German Pinscher for jumping up on you today, then allow it to happen tomorrow by greeting him with hugs and kisses. As you have learned by now, consistency is critical to all puppy lessons.

For starters, try turning your back as soon as the puppy jumps. Jumping up is a means of gaining your attention and, if the pup can't see your face, he may get discouraged and learn that he loses eye contact with his beloved master when he jumps up.

Leash corrections also work, and most puppies respond well to a leash tug if they jump. Grasp the leash close to the puppy's collar and give a quick tug downward, using the command "Off." Do not use the word "Down," since "Down" is used to teach the puppy to lie down, which is a separate action that he will learn during his education in the basic commands. As soon as the puppy has backed off, tell him to sit and immediately praise him for doing so. This will take many repetitions and won't be accomplished quickly, so don't get discouraged or give up; you must be even more persistent than your puppy.

Another method used for jump correction is the spritzer bottle. Fill a spray bottle with water mixed with a bit of lemon juice or vinegar. As soon as the puppy jumps, command him "Off" and spritz him with the water mixture. Of course, that means having the spray bottle handy whenever or wherever jumping usually happens.

Yet another method to discourage jumping is grasping the puppy's paws and holding them gently but firmly until he struggles to get away. Wait a brief moment or two, then release his paws and give him a command to sit. He should eventually learn that jumping gets him into an

If you don't want your German Pinscher jumping up as an adult it is important not to let him do so as a puppy.

DIGGING OUT

Some dogs love to dig. Others wouldn't think of it. Digging is considered "self-rewarding behavior" because it's fun! Of all the digging solutions offered by the experts, most are only marginally successful and none is guaranteed to work. The best cure is prevention, which means removing the dog from the offending site when he digs as well as distracting him when you catch him digging so that he turns his attentions elsewhere. That means that you have to supervise your dog's yard time. An unsupervised digger can create havoc with your landscaping or, worse, run away!

uncomfortable predicament.

Children are major victims of puppy jumping, since puppies view little people as ready targets for jumping up as well as nipping. If your children (or their friends) are unable to dispense jump corrections, you will have to intervene and handle it for them.

Important to prevention is also knowing what you should not do. Never kick your German Pinscher (for any reason, not just for jumping) or knock him in the chest with your knee. That maneuver could actually harm your puppy. Vets can tell you stories about puppies who suffered broken bones after being banged about when they jumped up.

PUPPY WHINING

Puppies often cry and whine, just as infants and little children do. It's their way of telling us that they are lonely or in need of attention. Your puppy will miss his littermates and will feel insecure when he is left alone. You may be out of the house or just in another room, but he will still feel alone. During these times, the puppy's crate should be his personal comfort station, a place all his own where he can feel safe and secure. Once he learns that being alone is okay and not something to be feared, he will settle down without crying or objecting. You might want to leave a radio on while he is crated, as the sound of human voices can be soothing and will give the impression that people are around.

Give your puppy a favorite safe cuddly toy or chew toy to

entertain him whenever he is crated. You will both be happier: the puppy because he is safe in his den and you because he is quiet, safe and not getting into puppy escapades that can wreak havoc in your house or cause him danger.

To make sure that your puppy will always view his crate as a safe and cozy place, never, ever use the crate as punishment. That's the best way to turn the crate into a negative place that the pup will want to avoid. Sure, you can use the crate for your own peace of mind if your puppy is getting into trouble and needs some "time out." Just don't let him know that. Never scold the pup and immediately place him into the crate. Count to ten, give him a couple of hugs and maybe a treat, then scoot him into his crate.

It's also important not to make a big fuss when he is released from the crate. That will make getting out of the crate more appealing than being in the crate, which is just the opposite of what you are trying to achieve.

COUNTER SURFING

What we like to call "counter surfing" is a normal extension of jumping and usually starts to happen as soon as a puppy realizes that he is big enough to stand on his hind legs and investigate the good stuff on the kitchen counter or the coffee table. Once again, you have to be there to prevent it! As soon as you see your German Pinscher even start to raise himself up, startle him with a sharp "No!" or "Aaahh, aaahh!" If he succeeds and manages to get one or both

---

HEART-HEALTHY

In this modern age of ever-improving cardio-care, no doctor or scientist can dispute the advantages of owning a dog to lower a person's risk of heart disease. Studies have proven that petting a dog, walking a dog and grooming a dog all show positive results toward lowering your blood pressure. The simple routine of exercising your dog—going outside with the dog and walking, jogging or playing catch—is heart-healthy in and of itself. If you are normally less active than your physician thinks you should be, adopting a dog may be a smart option to improve your own quality of life as well as that of another creature.

paws on the forbidden surface, smack those paws (firmly but gently) and tell him "Off!" As soon as he's back on all four paws, command him to sit and praise at once.

For surf prevention, make sure to keep any tempting treats or edibles out of reach, where your German Pinscher can't see or smell them. It's the old rule of prevention yet again.

FOOD GUARDING
Some dogs are picky eaters; others seem to inhale their food without chewing it. Occasionally the true "chow hound" will become protective of his food, which is one dangerous step toward other aggressive behaviors. Food guarding is obvious: your puppy will growl, snarl or even attempt to bite you if you approach his food bowl or

It is important not to leave food within the reach of your German Pinscher because he will surely help himself.

put your hand into his pan while he's eating.

This behavior is not acceptable and very preventable! If your puppy is an especially voracious eater, sit next to him occasionally while he eats and dangle your fingers in his food bowl. Don't feed him in a corner, where he could feel possessive of his eating space. Rather, place his food bowl in an open area of your kitchen where you are in close proximity. Occasionally remove his food in mid-meal, tell him he's a good boy and return his bowl.

If your pup becomes possessive of his food, look for other signs of future aggression, like guarding his favorite toys or refusing to obey obedience commands that he knows. Consult an obedience trainer for help in reinforcing obedience so your German Pinscher will fully understand that *you* are the boss.

DOMESTIC SQUABBLES
How well your new German Pinscher will get along with an older dog who has squatter's rights depends largely on the individual dogs. Like people, some dogs are more gregarious than others and will enjoy having a furry friend to play with. Others will not be thrilled at the prospect of sharing their dog space with another canine.

It's best to introduce the dogs

to each other on neutral ground, away from home, so the resident dog won't feel so possessive. Keep both the puppy and adult on loose leads (loose is very important, as a tight lead sends negative signals and can intimidate either dog) and allow them to sniff and do their doggie things. A few raised hackles are normal, with the older dog pawing at the youngster. Let the two work things out between them unless you see signs of real aggression, such as deep growls or curled lips and serious snarls. You may have to keep them separated until the veteran gets used to the new family member, often after the pup has outgrown the silly puppy stage and is more mature in stature. Take precautions to make sure that the puppy does not become frightened by

Two dogs in one home can become best buddies if properly introduced and supervised as their friendship develops.

the older dog's behavior.

Whatever happens, it's important to make your resident dog feel secure. (Jealousy is normal among dogs, too!) Pay extra attention to the older dog: feed him first, hug him first and don't insist he share his toys or space with the new pup until he's ready. If the two are still at odds months later, consult an obedience professional for advice.

Cat introductions are a different story. Being agile and independent creatures, cats will scoot to high places, out of the puppy's reach. A cat might even tease the puppy and cuff him from above when the pup comes within paw's reach. German Pinschers and cats can get along in a home environment, although you always have to keep the Pinscher's chase instinct in mind.

MEET AND MINGLE

Puppies need to meet people and see the world if they are to grow up confident and unafraid. Take your puppy with you on everyday outings and errands. On-lead walks around the neighborhood and to the park offer the pup good exposure to the goings-on of his new human world. Avoid areas frequented by other dogs until your puppy has had his full round of puppy shots; ask your vet when your pup will be properly protected. Arrange for your puppy to meet new people of all ages every week.

PROPER CARE OF YOUR

GERMAN PINSCHER

Adding a German Pinscher to your household means adding a new family member who will need your care each and every day. When your German Pinscher pup first comes home, you will start a routine with him so that, as he grows up, your dog will have a daily schedule just as you do. The aspects of your dog's daily care will likewise become regular parts of your day, so you'll both have a new schedule. Dogs learn by consistency and thrive on routine: regular times for meals, exercise, grooming and potty trips are just as important for your dog as they are for you. Your dog's schedule will depend much on your family's

This German Pinscher and his Miniature Pinscher buddy may both like to eat, but that doesn't mean they should be fed the same food. There are many kinds of foods available, with types formulated for dogs of various sizes and ages.

THE DARK SIDE OF CHOCOLATE

From a tiny chip to a giant rabbit, chocolate—in any form—is not your dog's friend. Whether it's an Oreo® cookie, a Snickers® bar or even a couple of M&M's®, you should avoid these items with your dog. You are also well advised to avoid any bone toy that is made out of fake chocolate or any treat made of carob—anything that encourages your dog to become a "chocoholic" can't be helpful. Before you toss your pooch half of your candy bar, consider that as little as a single ounce of chocolate can poison a 30-pound dog. Theobromine, like caffeine, is a methylxanthine and occurs naturally in cocoa beans. Dogs metabolize theobromine very slowly, and its effect on the dog can be serious, harming the heart, kidneys and central nervous system. Dark or semi-sweet chocolate is even worse than milk chocolate, and baking chocolate and cocoa mix are by far the worst.

daily routine, but remember that you now have a new member of the family who is part of your day every day.

FEEDING

Feeding your dog the best diet is based on various factors, including age, activity level, overall condition and size of breed. When you visit the breeder, he will share with you his advice about the proper diet for your dog based on his experience with the breed and the foods with which he has had success. Likewise, your vet will be a helpful source of advice throughout the dog's life

Mother's milk is best for German Pinscher pups during their first few weeks of life. They will eventually be introduced to solid food as part of the weaning process.

and will aid you in planning a diet for optimal health.

FEEDING THE PUPPY

Of course, your pup's very first food will be his dam's milk. There may be special situations in which pups fail to nurse, necessitating that the breeder hand-feed them with a formula, but for the most part pups spend the first weeks of life nursing from their dam. The breeder weans the pups by gradually introducing solid foods and decreasing the milk meals. Pups may even start themselves off on the weaning process, albeit inadvertently, if they snatch bites from their mom's food bowl.

By the time the pups are ready for new homes, they are fully weaned and eating a good puppy food. As a new owner, you may be thinking, "Great! The breeder has taken care of the hard part." Not so fast.

THE BOVINE CANINE

Does your dog's grazing in the back yard have you wondering whether he's actually a farm animal in disguise? Many owners have noticed their dogs eating grass and wonder why! It is thought that dogs might eat grass to settle their stomachs or to relieve upset tummies. Even cats have been known to eat grass for the same reasons! Stomach upset can be caused by various things, including poor digestion and parasites.

Unfortunately, while the grass may make dogs feel better very temporarily, often they vomit shortly after eating it, as grass can be irritating to a dog's stomach lining. Even worse, who knows what he is ingesting along with the grass? He could be swallowing insects, germs or parasites, thus perpetuating the problem. Grass-eating should be discouraged when you catch the dog in the act, and a trip to the vet to determine the underlying cause is in order.

An adult German Pinscher can be maintained fairly easily on a complete formula dog food.

A puppy's first year of life is the time when much of his growth and development takes place. This is a delicate time, and diet plays a huge role in proper skeletal and muscular formation. Improper diet and exercise habits can lead to damaging problems that will compromise the dog's health and movement for his entire life. That being said, new owners should not worry needlessly. With the myriad types of food formulated specifically for growing pups of different-sized breeds, dog-food manufacturers have taken much of the guesswork out of feeding your puppy well. Since growth-food formulas are designed to provide the nutrition that a growing puppy needs, it is unnecessary and, in fact, can prove harmful to add supplements to the diet. Research has shown that too much of certain vitamin supplements and minerals predispose a dog to skeletal

problems. It's by no means a case of "if a little is good, a lot is better." At every stage of your dog's life, too much or too little in the way of nutrients can be harmful, which is why a manufactured complete food is the easiest way to know that your dog is getting what he needs.

Because of a young pup's small body and accordingly small digestive system, his daily portion will be divided up into small meals throughout the day. This can mean starting off with three or more

SWITCHING FOODS
There are certain times in a dog's life when it becomes necessary to switch his food; for example, from puppy to adult food and then from adult to senior-dog food. Additionally, you may decide to feed your pup a different type of food from what he received from the breeder, and there may be "emergency" situations in which you can't find your dog's normal brand and have to offer something else temporarily. Anytime a change is made, for whatever reason, the switch must be done gradually. You don't want to upset the dog's stomach or end up with a picky eater who refuses to eat something new. A tried-and-true approach is, over the course of about a week, to mix a little of the new food in with the old, increasing the proportion of new to old as the days progress. At the end of the week, you'll be feeding his regular portions of the new food, and he will barely notice the change.

BARF THE WAY TO BETTER HEALTH

That's Biologically Appropriate Raw Food for your dog, as designed and trademarked by Dr. Ian Billinghurst. An alternative to feeding commercially prepared dog food from bags or cans that are known to contain numerous additives and preservatives, this diet aims to increase the longevity, overall health and reproductive abilities of dogs. The BARF diet is based on the feeding habits of wild or feral animals and thus includes whole raw animal- and plant-based foods as well as bones. In theory, BARF mimics the natural diets of dogs and contains muscle meat, bone, fat and organ meat plus vegetable matter. Many owners are very successful with the diet and others are not. Next time you visit your vet, ask him what he knows about BARF.

proportionately more food per body weight than their adult counterparts, but a pup should never be allowed to gain excess weight. Dogs of all ages should be kept in proper body condition, but extra weight can strain a pup's developing frame, causing skeletal problems.

Watch your pup's weight as he grows and, if the recommended amounts seem to be too much or too little for your pup, consult the vet about appropriate dietary changes. Keep in mind that treats, although small, can quickly add up throughout the day, contributing unnecessary calories. Treats are fine when used prudently; opt for dog treats specially formulated to be healthy or for nutritious snacks like small pieces of cheese or cooked chicken.

FEEDING THE ADULT DOG

For the adult (meaning physically mature) dog, feeding properly is about maintenance, not growth.

meals a day and decreasing the number of meals as the pup matures. For the adult, dividing the day's food into two meals on a morning/evening schedule is healthier for the dog's digestion; one large daily portion can be harmful.

Regarding the feeding schedule, feeding the pup at the same times and in the same place each day is important for both housebreaking purposes and establishing the dog's everyday routine. As for the amount to feed, growing puppies generally need

When outdoors, make sure your dog has access to water, especially during the hot summer months.

This adult German Pinscher is well past teething but he hasn't outgrown a little mischief-making.

Again, correct weight is a concern. Your dog should appear fit and should have an evident "waist." His ribs should not be protruding (a sign of being underweight), but they should be covered by only a slight layer of fat. Under normal circumstances, an adult dog can be maintained fairly easily with a high-quality nutritionally complete adult-formula food.

Factor treats into your dog's overall daily caloric intake, and avoid offering table scraps. Certain "people foods," like chocolate, onions, nuts, raisins, grapes and large amounts of garlic, are toxic to dogs. Overweight dogs are more prone to health problems. Research has even shown that obesity takes years off a dog's life. With that in mind, resist the urge to overfeed and over-treat. Don't make unnecessary additions to your dog's diet, whether with tidbits or with extra vitamins and minerals.

The amount of food needed for proper maintenance will vary depending on the individual dog's activity level, but you will be able to tell whether the daily portions are keeping him in good shape. With the wide variety of good complete foods available, choosing what to feed is largely a matter of personal preference. Just as with the puppy, the adult dog should have consistency in his mealtimes and feeding place. In addition to a consistent routine,

DIET DON'TS

- Got milk? Don't give it to your dog! Dogs cannot tolerate large quantities of cows' milk, as they do not have the enzymes to digest lactose.
- You may have heard of dog owners who add raw eggs to their dogs' food for a shiny coat or to make the food more palatable, but consumption of raw eggs too often can cause a deficiency of the vitamin biotin.
- Avoid feeding table scraps, as they will upset the balance of the dog's complete food. Additionally, fatty or highly seasoned foods can cause upset canine stomachs.
- Raw meat can contain parasites. Be fully informed if you choose to feed raw food.
- Vitamin A toxicity in dogs can be caused by too much raw liver, especially if the dog already gets enough vitamin A in his balanced diet, which should be the case.
- Bones like chicken, pork chop and other soft bones are not suitable, as they easily splinter.

regular mealtimes also allow the owner to see how much his dog is eating. If the dog seems never to be satisfied or, likewise, becomes uninterested in his food, the owner will know right away that something is wrong and can consult the vet.

DIETS FOR THE AGING DOG

A good rule of thumb is that once a dog has reached around 75% of his expected lifespan, he has reached "senior citizen" or geriatric status. Your German Pinscher will be considered a senior at about 9 years of age; this is a long-lived breed with a projected lifespan of about 12–14 years or even longer.

What does aging have to do with your dog's diet? No, he won't get a discount at the local diner's early-bird special. Yes, he will require some dietary changes to accommodate the changes that come along with increased age. One change is that the older dog's dietary needs become more similar to that of a puppy. Specifically, dogs can metabolize more protein as youngsters and seniors than in the adult-maintenance stage. Discuss with your vet whether you need to switch to a higher-protein or senior-formulated food or whether your current adult-dog food contains sufficient nutrition for the senior.

Watching the dog's weight remains essential, even more so in

FRESH OPTIONS
While a packaged dog food, formulated to provide complete nutrition and proper balance, is no doubt the most convenient way to feed your dog well, some owners prefer to take their dogs' food preparation into their own hands (and kitchens). Homemade fresh-food diets and raw-food diets certainly have their proponents in the dog world. Those who feed the raw, natural diet of the wild do not believe that a dog's food should be cooked and that dogs should not be fed grains of any type. They feel that raw-food diets keep their dogs in optimal physical and temperamental shape, with wonderfully healthy coats and no allergy problems. Those who cook for their dogs typically do so because they do not like the additives and preservatives that go into commercial foods. Many homemade diets are based on a balance of cooked meat, vegetables and grains. If you choose to create your dog's diet on your own, you must thoroughly educate yourself about how to do this correctly for proper nutrition. Not all vets are knowledgeable about these feeding methods, nor will all vets recommend them, so it's best to talk with those vets, breeders, nutrition experts and owners who are experienced and have been successful with fresh- or raw-food diets in dogs.

the senior stage. Older dogs are already more vulnerable to illness, and obesity only contributes to

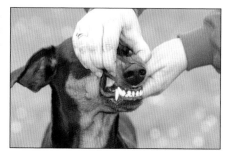

Brush your dog's teeth as frequently as possible. A daily brushing is ideal, but once a week is more usual.

their susceptibility to problems. As the older dog becomes less active and thus exercises less, his regular portions may cause him to gain weight. At this point, you may consider decreasing his daily food intake or switching to a reduced-calorie food. As with other changes, you should consult your vet for advice.

TYPES OF FOOD AND READING THE LABEL

When selecting the type of food to feed your dog, it is important to check out the label for ingredients. Many dry-food products have soybean, corn or rice as the main ingredient. The main ingredient will be listed first on the label, with the rest of the ingredients following in descending order according to their proportion in the food. While these types of dry food are popular, you should look into dry foods based on meat or fish. These are better-quality foods and thus higher priced. However, they may be just as economical in the long run, because studies have shown that it takes less of the higher-quality

foods to maintain a dog.

Comparing the various types of food, dry, canned and semi-moist, dry foods contain the least amount of water and canned foods the most. Proportionately, dry foods are the most calorie- and nutrient-dense, which means that you need more of a canned food product to supply the same amount of nutrition. In households with breeds of disparate sizes, the canned/dry/semi-moist question can be of special importance. Larger breeds obviously eat more than smaller ones and thus in general do better on dry foods, but smaller breeds do fine on canned foods and require "small bite" formulations to protect their small mouths and teeth if fed dry foods. So if you have breeds of different

JUST ADD MEAT

An organic alternative to the traditional dog kibble or canned food comes in the form of grain-based feeds. These dry cereal-type products consist of oat and rye flakes, corn meal, wheat germ, dried kelp and other natural ingredients. The manufacturers recommend that the food be mixed with meat in a ratio of two parts grain to one part meat. As an alternative to fresh meat, investigate freeze-dried meat and fermented meat products, which makers claim are more nutritious and digestible for dogs.

sizes in your household, consider both your own preferences and what your dogs like to eat, but generally think canned for the little guys and dry or semi-moist for everyone else. You may find success mixing the food types as well. Water is important for all dogs, but even more so for those fed dry foods, as there is no high water content in their food.

There are strict controls that regulate the nutritional content of dog food, and a food has to meet the minimum requirements in order to be considered "complete and balanced." It is important that you choose such a food for your dog, so check the label to be sure that your chosen food meets the requirements. If not, look for a food that clearly states on the label that it is formulated to be complete and balanced for your dog's particular stage of life.

Recommendations for amounts to feed will also be indicated on the label. You should also ask your vet about proper food portions, and you will keep an eye on your dog's condition to see whether the recommended amounts are adequate. If he becomes over- or underweight, you will need to make adjustments; this also would be a good time to consult your vet.

The food label may also make feeding suggestions, such as whether moistening a dry-food product is recommended. Sometimes a splash of water will

NOT HUNGRY?
No dog in his right mind would turn down his dinner, would he? If you notice that your dog has lost interest in his food, there could be any number of causes. Dental problems are a common cause of appetite loss, one that is often overlooked. If your dog has a toothache, a loose tooth or sore gums from infection, chances are it doesn't feel so good to chew. Think about when you've had a toothache! If your dog does not approach the food bowl with his usual enthusiasm, look inside his mouth for signs of a problem. Whatever the cause, you'll want to consult your vet so that your chow hound can get back to his happy, hungry self as soon as possible.

make the food more palatable for the dog and even enhance the flavor. Don't be overwhelmed by the many factors that go into feeding your dog. Manufacturers of complete and balanced foods make it easy, and once you find the right food, amount and schedule for your German Pinscher, his daily feeding will be a matter of routine.

DON'T FORGET THE WATER!
Regardless of what type of food your dog eats, there's no doubt that he needs plenty of water. Fresh cold water in a clean bowl should be available to your dog. There are special circumstances, such as during puppy housebreaking, when

The German Pinscher may not be a natural water dog, but Falcon's curiosity is drawing him to investigate the ocean.

This German Pinscher enjoys a romp in the snow.

you will want to monitor your pup's water intake so that you will be able to predict when he will need to relieve himself, but water must be available to him nonetheless. Water is essential for hydration and proper body function just as it is in humans.

You will get to know how much your dog typically drinks in a day. Of course, in the heat or if exercising vigorously, he will be more thirsty and will drink more. However, if he begins to drink noticeably more water for no apparent reason, this could signal any of various problems, and you are advised to consult your vet.

Water is the best drink for dogs. Some owners are tempted to give milk from time to time or to moisten dry food with milk, but dogs do not have the enzymes necessary to digest the lactose in milk, which is much different from the milk that nursing puppies receive. Therefore stick with clean fresh water to quench your dog's thirst.

EXERCISE

We all know the importance of exercise for humans, so it should come as no surprise that it is essential for our canine friends as well. Now, regardless of your own level of fitness, get ready to assume the role of personal trainer for your dog. It's not as hard as it sounds, and it will have health benefits for you, too.

Just as with anything else you do with your dog, you must set a routine for his exercise. It's the same as your daily morning run before work or never missing the 7 p.m. aerobics class. If you plan it and get into the habit of actually doing it, it will become just another part of your day. Think of it as making daily exercise appointments with your dog, and stick to your schedule.

TWO'S COMPANY

One method of increasing your adult dog's exercise plan is to adopt a second dog. If your dog is well socialized, he will hopefully enjoy the company of a new canine pal and soon the two will be giving each other lots of activity and exercise as they play, romp and explore together. Most owners agree that two dogs are hardly much more work than one. If you cannot afford a second dog, get together with a friend or neighbor who has a well-trained dog that your dog gets along well with.

As a rule, dogs in normal health should have at least a half-hour of activity each day. Dogs with health or orthopedic problems may have specific limitations, so their exercise plans are best devised with the help of a vet. For healthy dogs, there are many ways to fit 30 minutes of activity into your day. Depending on your schedule, you may plan a 15-minute walk or activity session in the morning and again in the evening, or do it all at once in a half-hour session each day. Walking is the most popular way to exercise a dog (it's good for you, too!); other suggestions include retrieving games, jogging, disc-catching or other active games with his toys. If you have a safe body of water nearby and a dog that likes to swim, swimming is an excellent form of exercise for dogs, putting no stress on his

Your German Pinscher should remain on lead if exercising outdoors in an area that does not have adequate fencing.

Introduce your German Pinscher to the grooming process as a puppy and he will learn to tolerate it as an adult.

some of them never seem to tire. They will enjoy time spent with their owners doing things together.

Regardless of your dog's condition and activity level, exercise offers benefits to all dogs and owners. Consider the fact that dogs who are kept active are more stimulated both physically and mentally, meaning that they are less likely to become bored and lapse into destructive behavior. Also consider the benefits of one-on-one time with your dog every day, continually strengthening the bond between the two of you. Furthermore, exercising together will improve health and longevity for both of you. You both need exercise, and now you and your dog have a workout partner and motivator!

frame. Of course, having a German Pinscher that likes to swim would be an odd occurrence, because this breed definitely is no lover of water in any form other than potable.

On that note, some precautions should be taken with a puppy's exercise. During his first year, when he is growing and developing, your German Pinscher should not be subject to activity that stresses his body. Short walks at a comfortable pace and play sessions in the yard are good for a growing pup, and his exercise can be increased as he grows up.

For overweight dogs, dietary changes and activity will help the goal of weight loss. (Sound familiar?) While they should of course be encouraged to be active, remember not to overdo it, as the excess weight is already putting strain on his vital organs and bones. As for highly active dogs,

GROOMING

BRUSHING
Being a short-haired, smooth-coated dog, the German Pinscher needs very little grooming. A good wipe-over, at least once a week, with a hound glove, chamois leather or velvet cloth will remove any dead hairs and keep carpets and furniture virtually hair-free. German Pinschers shed very little hair in any case. Some do not enjoy the grooming process, so begin acclimating the puppy to the routine right away. In time, your puppy will tolerate the regimen. You can be glad that your Pinscher

A German Pinscher will require little effort to remain a handsome dog. Here is Ch. Blue Banner's High Noon CD, AXP, AJP looking sharp. Owner Betsy Spilis.

German Pinschers also know how to relax after a hard day. Blue Banner's Magnum, an obedience dog owned by Debbie Kaminsky, takes a break by the pool.

isn't a Poodle and doesn't require hours and hours of primping and trimming. Yours is a wash-and-wear kind of canine.

BATHING

In general, dogs need to be bathed only a few times a year, possibly more often if your dog gets into something messy or if he starts to smell like a dog. Show dogs are usually bathed before every show, which could be as frequent as weekly, although this depends on the owner. Bathing too frequently can have negative effects on the skin and coat, removing natural oils and causing dryness.

If you give your dog his first bath when he is young, he will become accustomed to the process. Wrestling a dog into the tub or chasing a freshly shampooed dog who has escaped from the bath will be no fun! Most dogs don't naturally enjoy their baths, but you at least want yours to cooperate with you.

Before bathing the dog, have the items you'll need close at hand. First, decide where you will bathe the dog. You should have a tub or basin with a non-slip surface. Puppies can even be bathed in a sink. In warm weather, some like to use a portable pool in the yard, although you'll want to make sure your dog doesn't head for the nearest dirt pile following his bath! You will also need a hose or shower spray to wet the coat thoroughly, a shampoo formulated for dogs and several absorbent towels. Human shampoos are too harsh for dogs' coats and will dry them out.

Before wetting the dog, give him a brush-through to remove any dead hair, dirt and mats. Make sure he is at ease in the tub and have the water at a comfortable temperature. Begin bathing by wetting the coat all the way down to the skin.

Dogs that exercise regularly on hard pavement will wear their nails down naturally and require clipping less often than dogs that spend time only on grass or indoors.

THE MONTHLY GRIND

If your dog doesn't like the feeling of nail clippers or if you're not comfortable using them, you may wish to try an electric nail grinder. This tool has a small sandpaper disc on the end that rotates to grind the nails down. Some feel that using a grinder reduces the risk of cutting into the quick; this can be true if the tool is used properly. Usually you will be able to tell where the quick is before you get to it. A benefit of the grinder is that it creates a smooth finish on the nails so that there are no ragged edges.

Because the tool makes noise, your dog should be introduced to it before the actual grinding takes place. Turn it on and let your dog hear the noise; turn it off and let him inspect it with you holding it. Use the grinder gently, holding it firmly and progressing a little at a time until you reach the proper length. Look at the nail as you grind so that you do not go too short. Stop at any indication that you are nearing the quick. It will take a few sessions for both you and the puppy to get used to the grinder.

Massage in the shampoo, keeping it away from his face and eyes. Rinse him thoroughly, again avoiding the eyes and ears, as you don't want to get water into the ear canals. A thorough rinsing is important, as shampoo residue is drying and itchy to the dog. After rinsing, wrap him in a towel to absorb the initial moisture. You can finish drying with another dry towel; towel-drying is sufficient for the German Pinscher's short coat. You should keep the dog indoors and away from drafts until he is completely dry.

NAIL CLIPPING

Having their nails trimmed is not on many dogs' lists of favorite things to do. With this in mind, you will need to accustom your puppy to the procedure at a young age so that he will sit still (well, as still as he can) for his pedicures. Long nails can cause the dog's feet to spread, which is not good for him; likewise, long nails can hurt if they unintentionally scratch, not good for you!

Some dogs' nails are worn down naturally by regular walking on hard surfaces, so the frequency with which you clip depends on your individual dog. Look at his nails from time to time and clip as needed; a good way to know when it's time for a trim is if you hear your dog clicking as he walks across the floor.

There are several types of nail clippers and even electric nail-grinding tools made for dogs. First we'll discuss using the clipper. To start, have your clipper ready and some doggie treats on hand. You want your pup to view his nail-clipping sessions in a positive light, and what better way to convince him than with food? You may want to enlist the help of an assistant to comfort the pup and offer treats as you concentrate on the clipping itself. The guillotine-type clipper is thought of by many as the easiest type to use; the nail tip is inserted into the opening, and blades on the top and bottom snip it off in one clip.

Start by grasping the pup's paw; a little pressure on the foot pad causes the nail to extend, making it easier to clip. Clip off a little at a time. If you can see the

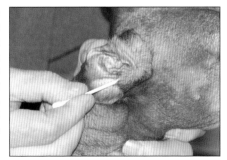

It is better to wipe your dog's ears clean with cotton balls than to probe them with a cotton swab, shown here, which could harm the inner ear.

"quick," which is a blood vessel that runs through each nail, you will know how much to trim, as you do not want to cut into the quick. On that note, if you do cut the quick, which will cause bleeding, you can stem the flow of blood with a styptic pencil or other clotting agent. If you mistakenly nip the quick, do not panic or fuss, as this will cause the pup to be afraid. Simply reassure the pup, stop the bleeding and move on to the next nail. Don't be discouraged; you will become a professional canine pedicurist with practice.

You may or may not be able to see the quick, so it's best to just clip off a small bit at a time. If you see a dark dot in the center of the nail, this is the quick and your cue to stop clipping. Tell the puppy he's a "good boy" and offer a piece of treat with each nail. You can also use nail-clipping time to examine the footpads, making sure that they are not dry and cracked and that nothing has become embedded in them.

The nail grinder, the other choice, is many owners' first choice. Accustoming the puppy to the sound of the grinder and sensation of the buzz presents fewer challenges than the clipper, and there's no chance of cutting through the quick. Use the grinder on a low setting and always talk soothingly to your dog. He won't mind his salon visit, and he'll have nicely polished nails as well.

THE EARS KNOW

Examining your puppy's ears helps ensure good internal health. The ears are the eyes to the dog's innards! Begin handling your puppy's ears when he's still young so that he doesn't protest every time you lift a flap or touch his ears. Yeast and bacteria are two of the culprits that you can detect by examining the ear. You will notice a strong, often foul, odor, debris, redness or some kind of discharge. All of these point to health problems that can worsen over time. Additionally, you are on the lookout for wax accumulation, ear mites and other tiny bothersome parasites and their even tinier droppings. You may have to pluck hair with tweezers in order to have a better view into the dog's ears, but this is painless if done carefully.

EAR CLEANING

While keeping your dog's ears clean unfortunately will not cause him to "hear" your commands any better, it will protect him from ear infection and ear-mite infestation. In addition, a dog's ears are vulnerable to waxy build-up and to collecting foreign matter from the outdoors. Look in your dog's ears regularly to ensure that they look pink, clean and otherwise healthy. Even if they look fine, an odor in the ears signals a problem and means it's time to call the vet.

A dog's ears should be cleaned

regularly; once a week is suggested, and you can do this along with your regular brushing. Using a cotton ball or pad, and never probing into the ear canal, wipe the ear gently. You can use an ear-cleansing liquid or powder available from your vet or pet-supply store; alternatively, you might prefer to use homemade solutions with ingredients like white vinegar or hydrogen peroxide diluted with water. Ask your vet about home remedies before you attempt to concoct something on your own.

Keep your dog's ears free of excess hair by plucking it as needed. If done gently, this will be painless for the dog. Look for wax, brown droppings (a sign of ear mites), redness or any other abnormalities. At the first sign of a problem, contact your vet so that he can prescribe an appropriate medication.

EYE CARE

During grooming sessions, pay extra attention to the condition of your dog's eyes. If the area around the eyes is soiled or if tear staining has occurred, there are various cleaning agents made especially for this purpose. Look at the dog's eyes to make sure no debris has entered; dogs with large eyes and those who spend time outdoors are especially prone to this.

The signs of an eye infection are obvious: mucus, redness,

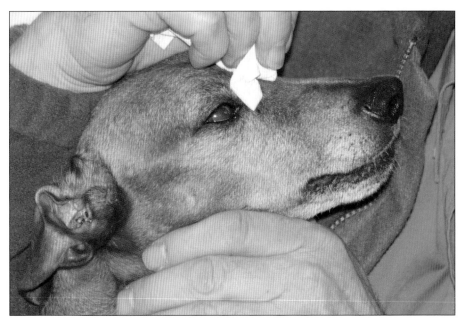

You can wipe around your dog's eyes with a soft cotton wipe to remove any debris that may accumulate there.

puffiness, scabs or other signs of irritation. If your dog's eyes become infected, the vet will likely prescribe an antibiotic ointment for treatment. If you notice signs of more serious problems, such as opacities in the eye, which usually indicate cataracts, consult the vet at once. Taking time to pay attention to your dog's eyes will alert you in the early stages of any problem so that you can get your dog treatment as soon as possible. You could save your dog's sight!

A CLEAN SMILE
Another essential part of grooming is brushing your dog's teeth and checking his overall oral condition. Studies show that around 80% of dogs experience dental problems

by two years of age, and the percentage is higher in older dogs. Therefore it is highly likely that your dog will have trouble with his teeth and gums unless you are proactive with home dental care.

The most common dental problem in dogs is plaque build-up. If not treated, this causes gum disease, infection and resultant

Yes, we brush our dogs' teeth too! Brushing keeps the teeth clean, the gums healthy and the breath fresh.

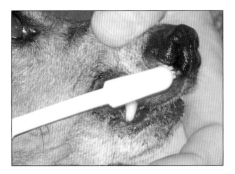

tooth loss. Bacteria from these infections spread throughout the body, affecting the vital organs. Do you need much more convincing to start brushing your dog's teeth? If so, take a good whiff of your dog's breath, and read on.

Fortunately, home dental care is rather easy and convenient for pet owners. Specially formulated canine toothpaste is easy to find. You should use one of these toothpastes, not a product for humans. Some doggie pastes are even available in flavors appealing to dogs. If your dog likes the flavor, he will tolerate the process better, making things much easier for you! Doggie toothbrushes come in different sizes and are designed to fit the contour of a canine mouth. Rubber fingertip brushes fit right on one of your fingers and have rubber nodes to clean the teeth and massage the gums. This may be easier to handle, as it is akin to rubbing your dog's teeth with your finger.

As with other grooming tasks, accustom your German Pinscher pup to his dental care early on. Start gently, for a few minutes at a time, so that he gets used to the feel of the brush and to your handling his mouth. Offer praise and petting so that he looks at tooth-care time as a time when he gets extra love and attention. The routine should become second nature; he may not like it, but he should at least tolerate it.

Aside from brushing, offer dental toys to your dog and feed crunchy biscuits, which help to minimize plaque. Rope toys have the added benefit of acting like floss as the dog chews. At your

PRESERVING THOSE PEARLY WHITES

What do you treasure more than the smile of your beloved canine pal? Brushing your dog's teeth is just as important as brushing your own. Neglecting your dog's teeth can lead to tooth loss, periodontal disease and inflamed gums, not to mention bad breath. Can you find the time to brush your dog's teeth every day? If not, you should do so once a week at the very least, though every day is truly ideal. Your vet should give your dog a thorough dental examination during his annual check-ups.

Pet shops sell terrific tooth-care devices, including specially designed toothbrushes, yummy toothpastes and finger-model brushes. You can use a human toothbrush with soft bristles, but never use human toothpastes, which can damage the dog's enamel. Baking soda is an alternative to doggie toothpastes, but your dog will be more receptive to canine toothpastes with the flavor of liver or hamburger. Make tooth care fun for your dog. Let him think that you're "horsing around" with his mouth. When brushing the dog's teeth, begin with the largest teeth (the canines) and proceed back toward the molars.

adult dog's yearly check-ups, the vet will likely perform a thorough tooth scraping as well as a complete check for any problems. Proper care of your dog's teeth will ensure that you will enjoy your dog's smile for many years to come. The next time your dog goes to give you a hello kiss, you'll be glad you spent the time caring for his teeth.

THE OTHER END

Dogs sometime have troubles with their anal glands, which are sacs located beside the anal vent. These should empty when a dog has normal bowel movements; if they don't, they can become full or impacted, causing discomfort. Owners often are alarmed to see their dogs scooting across the floor, dragging their behinds behind, but this is just a dog's attempt to empty the glands himself.

Some brave owners attempt to evacuate their dogs' anal glands themselves during grooming, but no one will tell you that this is a pleasant task! Thus many owners prefer to make the trip to the vet to have the vet take care of the problem; owners whose dogs visit a groomer can have this done by the groomer if he offers this as part of his services. Regardless, don't neglect the dog's other end in your home-care routine. Look for scooting, licking or other signs of discomfort "back

Kathy Dorwart taking a dog show break with Ch. Windamir's Vegas Des Charmettes.

there" to ascertain whether the anal glands need to be emptied.

IDENTIFICATION AND TRAVEL

ID FOR YOUR DOG

You love your German Pinscher and want to keep him safe. Of course you take every precaution to prevent his escaping from the yard or becoming lost or stolen. You have a sturdy high fence and you always keep your dog on lead when out and about in public places. If your dog is not properly identified, however, you are overlooking a major aspect of his safety. We hope to never be in a situation where our dog is missing, but we should practice prevention in the unfortunate case that this happens; identification greatly increases the chances of your dog's being returned to you.

There are several ways to identify your dog. First, the traditional dog tag should be a staple in your dog's wardrobe, attached to his everyday collar. Tags can be made of sturdy plastic and various metals and should include your contact information so that a person who finds the dog can get in touch with you right away to arrange his return. Many people today enjoy the wide range of decorative tags available, so have fun and create a tag to match your dog's personality. Of course, it is important that the tag stays on the collar, so have a secure "O" ring

WATER SHORTAGE

No matter how well behaved your dog is, bathing is always a project! Nothing can substitute for a good warm bath, but owners do have the option of giving their dogs "dry" baths. Pet shops sell excellent products, in both powder and spray forms, designed for spot-cleaning your dog. These dry shampoos are convenient for touch-up jobs when you don't have the time to bathe your dog in the traditional way.

Muddy feet, messy behinds and smelly coats can be spot-cleaned and deodorized with a "wet-nap"-style cleaner. On those days when your dog insists on rolling in fresh goose droppings and there's no time for a bath, a spot bath can save the day. These pre-moistened wipes are also handy for other grooming needs like wiping faces, ears and eyes and freshening tails and behinds.

attachment; you also can explore the type of tag that slides right onto the collar.

In addition to the identification tag, which every dog should wear even if identified by another method, two other forms of identification have become popular: microchipping and tattooing. In microchipping, a tiny scannable chip is painlessly inserted under the dog's skin. The number is registered to you so that, if your lost dog turns up at a clinic or shelter, the chip can be scanned to retrieve your contact information.

The advantage of the microchip is that it is a permanent form of ID, but there are some factors to consider. Several different companies make microchips, and not all are compatible with the others' scanning devices. It's best to find a company with a universal microchip that can be read by scanners made by other companies as well. It won't do any good to have the dog chipped if the information cannot be retrieved. Also, not every humane society, shelter and clinic is equipped with a scanner, although more and more facilities are equipping themselves. In fact, many shelters microchip dogs that they adopt out to new homes.

Because the microchip is not visible to the eye, the dog must wear a tag that states that he is microchipped so that whoever picks him up will know to have him scanned. He of course also should have a tag with your contact information no matter what. Humane societies and veterinary clinics offer microchipping service, which is usually very affordable.

Though less popular than microchipping, tattooing is another permanent method of ID for dogs. Most vets perform this service, and there are also clinics that perform dog tattooing. This is also an affordable procedure and one that will not cause much discomfort for the dog. It is best to put the tattoo in a visible area, such as the ear, to deter theft. It is sad to say that there are cases of dogs' being stolen and sold to research laboratories, but such laboratories will not accept tattooed dogs.

To ensure that the tattoo is

PET OR STRAY?

Besides the obvious benefit of providing your contact information to whoever finds your lost dog, an ID tag makes your dog more approachable and more likely to be recovered. A strange dog wandering the neighborhood without a collar and tags will look like a stray, while the collar and tags indicate that the dog is someone's pet. Even if the ID tags become detached from the collar, the collar alone will make a person more likely to pick up the dog.

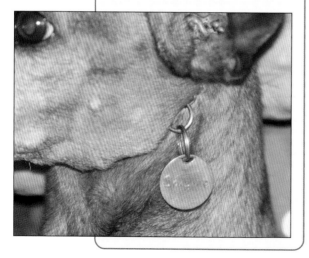

IF YOU FIND A LOST DOG

If you find a lost dog and want to help, here are some tips. First of all, the dog may act unpredictably, so assess the situation. If you feel uneasy, don't try to approach him. Instead, call the local police department or humane society. If the dog looks friendly and has a collar with an ID tag, approach him carefully. Squat down and extend a hand so that he can sniff it. Be gentle and speak in a friendly tone. Hopefully he will come near enough so that you can get the information from his tags. If he has no identification, and you can transport the dog, you can take him to a humane society or to your own home, though you should advise the local authorities and animal shelters that you have found a dog, as most owners will contact these agencies first if their dog is missing.

It's natural to want to rescue a stray or lost dog, so do what you can. After all, if your own dog ended up in the same situation, wouldn't you hope that someone else would take the time to help him?

If you find a badly injured animal with no identification, you have several things to think about. Taking him to an animal shelter does not necessarily mean that he will be all fixed up and ready to adopt; this depends on the individual shelter, so ask if and how they can help. If you choose to take the dog to a private vet, you must be ready to assume the costs of his treatment.

Your German Pinscher must always wear his identification tag, which should be securely attached to his collar and contain your current contact information.

effective in aiding your dog's return to you, the tattoo number must be registered with a national organization. That way, when someone finds a tattooed dog, a phone call to the registry will quickly match the dog with his owner.

HIT THE ROAD

Car travel with your German Pinscher may be limited to necessity only, such as trips to the vet, or you may bring your dog along almost everywhere you go. This will depend much on your individual dog and how he reacts to rides in the car. You can begin desensitizing your dog to car travel as a pup so that it's something that he's used to. Still, some dogs suffer from motion sickness. Your vet may prescribe a medication for this

if trips in the car pose a problem for your dog. At the very least, you will need to get him to the vet, so he will need to tolerate these trips with the least amount of hassle possible.

Start taking your pup on short trips, maybe just around the block to start. If he is fine with short trips, lengthen your rides a little at a time. Start to take him on your errands or just for drives around town. By this time it will be easy to tell whether your dog is a born traveler or would prefer staying at home when you are on the road.

Of course, safety is a concern for dogs in the car. First, he must travel securely, not left loose to roam about the car where he could be injured or distract the driver. A young pup can be held by a passenger initially but should soon graduate to a travel crate, which can be the same crate he uses in the home. Other options include a car harness (like a seat belt for dogs) and partitioning the back of the car with a gate made for this purpose.

Bring along what you will need for the dog. He should wear his collar and ID tags, of course, and you should bring his leash, water (and food if a long trip) and clean-up materials for potty breaks and in case of motion sickness. Always keep your dog on his leash when you make stops, and never leave him alone in the car. Many a dog has died from the heat inside a closed car; this does not take much time at all. A dog left alone inside a car can also be a target for thieves.

BOARDING

Today there are many options for dog owners who need someone to care for their dogs in certain circumstances. While many think of boarding their dogs as something to do when away on vacation, many others use the services of doggie "daycare" facilities, dropping their dogs off to spend the day while they are at work. Many of these facilities offer both long-term and daily care. Many go beyond just boarding and cater to all sorts of needs, with on-site grooming, veterinary care, training classes and even "web-cams" where owners can log onto the Internet and check out what their dogs are up to. Most dogs enjoy the activity and time spent with other dogs.

Before you need to use such a service, check out the ones in your area. Make visits to see the facilities, meet the staff, discuss fees and

available services and see whether this is a place where you think your dog will be happy. It is best to do your research in advance so that you're not stuck at the last minute, forced into making a rushed decision without knowing whether the kennel that you've chosen meets your standards. You also can check with your vet's office to see whether they offer boarding for their clients or can recommend a good kennel in the area.

The kennel will need to see proof of your dog's health records and vaccinations so as not to spread illness from dog to dog. Your dog also will need proper identification. Owners usually experience some separation anxiety the first time they have to leave their dog in someone else's care, so it's reassuring to know that the kennel you choose is run by experienced, caring, true dog people.

Do your research ahead of time if you need to board your dog. You want to be totally comfortable with the facility you choose.

TRAINING YOUR

GERMAN PINSCHER

BASIC TRAINING PRINCIPLES: PUPPY VS. ADULT

There's a big difference between training an adult dog and training a young puppy. With a young puppy, everything is new. At eight to ten weeks of age, he will be experiencing many things, and he has nothing with which to compare these experiences. Up to this point, he has been with his dam and littermates, not one-on-one with people except in his interactions with his breeder and visitors to the litter.

When you first bring the puppy home, he is eager to please you. This means that he accepts doing things your way. During the next couple of months, he will absorb the basis of everything he needs to know for the rest of his life. This early age is even referred to as the "sponge" stage. After that, for the next 18 months, it's up to you to reinforce good manners by building on the foundation that you've established. Once your puppy is reliable in basic commands and behavior and has reached the appropriate age, you may gradually introduce him to some

of the interesting sports, games and activities available to pet owners and their dogs.

Raising your puppy is a family affair. Each member of the family must know what rules to set forth for the puppy and how to use the same one-word commands to mean exactly the same thing every time. Even if yours is a large family, one person will soon be considered by the pup to be the leader, the Alpha person in his pack, the "boss" who must be obeyed. Often that highly regarded person turns out to be the one who feeds the puppy. Food ranks very high on the puppy's list of important things! That's why your puppy is rewarded with small treats along with verbal praise when he responds to you correctly. As the puppy learns to do what you want him to do, the food rewards are gradually eliminated and only the praise remains. If you were to keep up with the food treats, you could have two problems on your hands—an obese dog and a beggar.

Training begins the minute your German Pinscher puppy

steps through the doorway of your home, so don't make the mistake of putting the puppy on the floor and telling him by your actions to "Go for it! Run wild!" Even if this is your first puppy, you must act as if you know what you're doing: be the boss. An uncertain pup may be terrified to move, while a bold one will be ready to take you at your word and start plotting to destroy the house! Before you collected your puppy, you decided where his own special place would be, and that's where to put him when you first arrive home. Give him a house tour after he has investigated his area and had a nap and a bathroom "pit stop."

It's worth mentioning here that, if you've adopted an adult dog that is completely trained to your liking, lucky you! You're off the hook! However, if that dog spent his life up to this point in a kennel, or even in a good home but without any real training, be prepared to tackle the job ahead. A dog three years of age or older with no previous training cannot be blamed for not knowing what he was never taught. While the dog is trying to understand and learn your rules, at the same time he has to unlearn many of his previously self-taught habits and general view of the world.

Working with a professional trainer will speed up your progress with an adopted adult

WHO'S TRAINING WHOM?

Dog training is a black-and-white exercise. The correct response to a command must be absolute, and the trainer must insist on completely accurate responses from the dog. A trainer cannot command his dog to sit and then settle for the dog's melting into the down position. Often owners are so pleased that their dogs "did something" in response to a command that they just shrug and say, "OK, Down" even though they wanted the dog to sit. You want your dog to respond to the command without hesitation: he must respond at that moment and correctly every time.

CREATURES OF HABIT

Canine behaviorists and trainers aptly describe dogs as "creatures of habit," meaning that dogs respond to structure in their daily lives and welcome a routine. Do not interpret this to mean that dogs enjoy endless repetition in their training sessions. Dogs get bored just as humans do. Keep training sessions interesting and exciting. Vary the commands and the locations in which you practice. Give short breaks for play in between lessons. A bored student will never be the best performer in the class.

how he acts upon meeting other dogs. If he was not socialized with dogs as a puppy, this could be a major problem. This does not mean that he's a "bad" dog, a vicious dog or an aggressive dog; rather, it means that he has no idea how to read another dog's body language. There's no way for him to tell whether the other dog is a friend or foe. Survival instinct takes over, telling him to attack first and ask questions later. This definitely calls for professional help and, even then, may not be a behavior that can be corrected 100% reliably (or even at all). If you have a puppy, this is why it is so very important to introduce your young puppy properly to other puppies and "dog-friendly" adult dogs.

dog. You'll need patience, too. Some new rules may be close to impossible for the dog to accept. After all, he's been successful so far by doing everything his way! (Patience again.) He may agree with your instruction for a few days and then slip back into his old ways, so you must be just as consistent and understanding in your teaching as you would be with a puppy. (More patience needed yet again!) Your dog has to learn to pay attention to your voice, your family, the daily routine, new smells, new sounds and, in some cases, even a new climate.

One of the most important things to find out about a newly adopted adult dog is his reaction to children (yours and others), strangers and your friends, and

HOUSE-TRAINING

Dogs are tactility-oriented when it comes to house-training. In other words, they respond to the surface on which they are given approval to eliminate. The choice is yours (the dog's version is in parentheses): The lawn (including the neighbors' lawns)? A bare patch of earth under a tree (where people like to sit and relax in the summertime)? Concrete steps or patio (all sidewalks, garages and basement floors)? The curbside (watch out for cars)? A small area of crushed stone in a corner of the yard (mine!)? The latter is the best choice if you can manage it, because it will remain strictly for the dog's use and is easy to keep clean.

You can start out with paper-training indoors and switch over to an outdoor surface as the puppy matures and gains control over his need to eliminate. For the nay-sayers, don't worry—this won't mean that the dog will soil on every piece of newspaper lying around the house. You are training him to go outside, remember? Starting out by paper-training often is the only choice for a city dog.

WHEN YOUR PUPPY'S "GOT TO GO"

Your puppy's need to relieve himself is seemingly non-stop, but signs of improvement will be seen each week. From 8 to 10 weeks old, the puppy will have to be taken outside every time he wakes up, about 10 to 15 minutes after every meal and after every period of play—all day long, from first thing in the morning until his bedtime! That's a total of ten or more trips per day to teach the puppy where it's okay to relieve himself. With that schedule in mind, you can see that house-training a young puppy is not a part-time job. It requires someone to be home all day.

If that seems overwhelming or impossible, do a little planning. For example, plan to pick up your puppy at the start of a vacation period. If you can't get home in the middle of the day, plan to hire a dog-sitter or ask a neighbor to come over to take the pup outside, feed him his lunch and then take him out again about ten or so minutes after he's eaten. Also make arrangements with that or another person to be your "emergency" contact if you have to stay late on the job. Remind yourself—repeatedly—that this hectic schedule improves as the puppy gets older.

HOME WITHIN A HOME

Your German Pinscher puppy needs to be confined to one secure, puppy-proof area when no one is able to watch his every move. Generally the kitchen is the place of choice because the floor is washable. Likewise, it's a busy family area that will accustom the pup to a variety of noises, everything from pots and pans to the telephone, blender and dishwasher. He will also be enchanted by the smell of your cooking (and will never be critical when you burn something). An exercise pen (also called an "ex-pen," a puppy version of a playpen) within the room of choice is an excellent means of confinement for a young pup. He can see out and has a certain amount of space in which to run about, but he is safe from dangerous things like electrical cords, heating units, trash baskets or open kitchen-supply cabinets.

Place the pen where the puppy will not get a blast of heat or air conditioning.

In the pen, you can put a few toys, his bed (which can be his crate if the dimensions of pen and crate are compatible) and a few layers of newspaper in one small corner, just in case. A water bowl can be hung at a convenient height on the side of the ex-pen so it won't become a splashing pool for an innovative puppy. His food dish can go on the floor, near but not under the water bowl.

Crates are something that pet owners are at last getting used to for their dogs. Wild or domestic canines have always preferred to sleep in den-like safe spots, and that is exactly what the crate provides. How often have you seen adult dogs that choose to sleep under a table or chair even though they have full run of the house? It's the den connection.

In your "happy" voice, use the word "Crate" every time you put the pup into his den. If he's new to a crate, toss in a small biscuit for him to chase the first few times. At night, after he's been outside, he should sleep in his crate. The crate may be kept in his designated area at night or, if you want to be sure to hear those wake-up yips in the morning, put the crate in a corner of your bedroom. However, don't make any response whatsoever to whining or crying. If he's

completely ignored, he'll settle down and get to sleep.

Good bedding for a young puppy is an old folded bath towel or an old blanket, something that is easily washable and disposable if necessary ("accidents" will happen!). Never put newspaper in the puppy's crate. Also those old ideas about adding a clock to replace his mother's heartbeat, or a hot-water bottle to replace her warmth, are just that—old ideas. The clock could drive the puppy nuts, and the hot-water bottle could end up as a very soggy waterbed! An extremely good breeder would have introduced your puppy to the crate by letting two pups sleep together for a couple of nights, followed by several nights alone. How thankful you will be if you found that breeder!

Safe toys in the pup's crate or area will keep him occupied, but monitor their condition closely. Discard any toys that show signs of being chewed to bits. Squeaky parts, bits of stuffing or plastic or any other small pieces can cause intestinal blockage or possibly choking if swallowed.

PROGRESSING WITH POTTY-TRAINING
After you've taken your puppy out and he has relieved himself in the area you've selected, he can have some free time with the family as long as there is someone responsible for watching him.

That doesn't mean just someone in the same room who is watching TV or busy on the computer, but one person who is doing nothing other than keeping an eye on the pup, playing with him on the floor and helping him understand his position in the pack.

This first taste of freedom will let you begin to set the house rules. If you don't want the dog on the furniture, now is the time to prevent his first attempts to jump up onto the couch. The word to use in this case is "Off," not "Down." "Down" is the word you will use to teach the down position, which is something entirely different.

Most corrections at this stage come in the form of simply distracting the puppy. Instead of telling him "No" for "Don't chew the carpet," distract the chomping puppy with a toy and he'll forget about the carpet.

As you are playing with the pup, do not forget to watch him closely and pay attention to his body language. Whenever you see him begin to circle or sniff, take the puppy outside to relieve himself. If you are paper-training, put him back into his confined area on the newspapers. In either case, praise him as he eliminates while he actually is in the act of relieving himself. Three seconds after he has finished is too late! You'll be praising him for running toward you, picking up a toy or

LEASH TRAINING

House-training and leash training go hand in hand, literally. When taking your puppy outside to do his business, lead him there on his leash. Unless an emergency potty run is called for, do not whisk the puppy up into your arms and take him outside. If you have a fenced yard, you have the advantage of letting the puppy loose to go out, but it's better to put the dog on the leash and take him to his designated place in the yard until he is reliably house-trained. Taking the puppy for a walk is the best way to house-train a dog. The dog will associate the walk with his time to relieve himself, and the exercise of walking stimulates the dog's bowels and bladder. Dogs that are not trained to relieve themselves on a walk may hold it until they get back home, which of course defeats half the purpose of the walk.

whatever he may be doing at that moment, and that's not what you want to be praising him for.

POTTY COMMAND

Most dogs love to please their masters; there are no bounds to what dogs will do to make their owners happy. The potty command is a good example of this theory. If toileting on command makes the master happy, then more power to him. Puppies will obligingly piddle if it really makes their keepers smile. Some owners can be creative about which word they will use to command their dogs to relieve themselves. Some popular choices are "Potty," "Tinkle," "Piddle," "Let's go," "Hurry up" and "Toilet." Give the command every time your puppy goes into position and the puppy will begin to associate his business with the command.

Timing is a vital tool in all dog training. Use it.

Remove soiled newspapers immediately and replace them with clean ones. You may want to take a small piece of soiled paper and place it in the middle of the new clean papers, as the scent will attract him to that spot when it's time to go again. That scent attraction is why it's so important to clean up any messes made in the house by using a product specially made to eliminate the odor of dog urine and droppings. Regular household cleansers won't do the trick. Pet shops sell the best pet deodorizers. Invest in the largest container you can find.

Scent attraction eventually will lead your pup to his chosen spot outdoors; this is the basis of outdoor training. When you take your puppy outside to relieve himself, use a one-word command such as "Outside" or "Go-potty" (that's one word to the puppy!) as you pick him up and attach his leash. Then put him down in his area. If for any reason you can't carry him, snap the leash on quickly and lead him to his spot. Now comes the hard part—hard for you, that is. Just stand there until he urinates and defecates. Move him a few feet in one direction or another if he's just sitting there looking at you, but remember that this is neither playtime nor time for a walk. This is strictly a business trip! Then, as he circles and squats (remember your timing!), give him a quiet "Good dog" as praise. If you start to jump for joy, ecstatic over his performance, he'll do one of two things: either he will stop midstream, as it were, or he'll do it again for you—in the house—and expect you to be just as delighted!

Give him five minutes or so and, if he doesn't go in that time, take him back indoors to his confined area and try again in another ten minutes, or immediately if you see him sniffing and circling. By careful observation, you'll soon work out a successful schedule.

Accidents, by the way, are just that—accidents. Clean them up quickly and thoroughly, without comment, after the puppy has been taken outside to finish his business and then put back into his area or crate. If you witness an accident in progress, say "No!" in a stern voice and get the pup outdoors immediately. No punishment is needed. You and your puppy are just learning each other's language, and sometimes it's easy to miss a puppy's message. Chalk it up to experience and watch more closely from now on.

KEEPING THE PACK ORDERLY

Discipline is a form of training that brings order to life. For example, military discipline is what allows the soldiers in an

army to work as one. Discipline is a form of teaching and, in dogs, is the basis of how the successful pack operates. Each member knows his place in the pack and all respect the leader, or alpha dog. It is essential for your puppy that you establish this type of relationship, with you as the alpha, or leader. It is a form of social coexistence that all canines recognize and accept. Discipline, therefore, is never to be confused with punishment. When you teach your puppy how you want him to behave, and he behaves properly and you praise him for it, you are disciplining him with a form of positive reinforcement.

For a dog, rewards come in the form of praise, a smile, a cheerful tone of voice, a few friendly pats or a rub of the ears. Rewards are also small food

Male dogs tend to be more fixated on their toileting needs, frequently stopping at every vertical object to leave their special mark.

treats. Obviously, that does not mean bits of regular dog food. Instead, treats are very small bits of special things like cheese or pieces of soft dog treats. The idea is to reward the dog with something very small that he can taste and swallow, providing instant positive reinforcement. If he has to take time to chew the treat, by the time he is finished he will have forgotten what he did to earn it!

Your puppy should never be physically punished. The displeasure shown on your face and in your voice is sufficient to signal to the pup that he has done something wrong. He wants to please everyone higher up on the social ladder, especially his leader, so a scowl and harsh voice will take care of the error. Growling out the word "Shame!" when the pup is caught in the act of doing something wrong is better than the repetitive "No." Some dogs hear "No" so often that they begin to think it's their name! By the way, do not use the dog's name when you're correcting him. His name is reserved to get his attention for something pleasant about to take place.

There are punishments that have nothing to do with you. For example, your dog may think that chasing cats is one reason for his existence. You can try to stop it as much as you like but without success, because it's such fun for

the dog. But one good hissing, spitting swipe of a cat's claws across the dog's nose will put an end to the game forever. Intervene only when your dog's eyeball is seriously at risk. Cat scratches can cause permanent damage to an innocent but annoying puppy.

PUPPY KINDERGARTEN

Collar and Leash
Before you begin your German Pinscher puppy's education, he must be used to his collar and leash. Choose a collar for your

---

COME AND GET IT!

The come command is your dog's safety signal. Until he is 99% perfect in responding, don't use the come command if you cannot enforce it. Practice on leash with treats or squeakers, or whenever the dog is running to you. Never call him to come to you if he is to be corrected for a misdemeanor. Reward the dog with a treat and happy praise whenever he comes to you.

puppy that is secure, but not heavy or bulky. He won't enjoy training if he's uncomfortable. A flat buckle collar is fine for everyday wear and for initial puppy training. For older dogs, there are several types of training collars such as the martingale, which is a double loop that tightens slightly around the neck, or the head collar, which is similar to a horse's halter. Do not use a chain choke collar unless you have been specifically shown how to put it on and how to use it. Ask your breeder for recommendations on suitable training collars for your German Pinscher.

A lightweight 6-foot woven cotton or nylon training leash is preferred by most trainers because it is easy to fold up in your hand and comfortable to hold because there is a certain amount of give to it. There are lessons where the dog will start off 6 feet away from you at the end of the leash. The leash used to take the puppy outside to relieve himself is shorter because you don't want him to roam away from his area. The shorter leash will also be the one to use when you walk the puppy.

If you've been fortunate enough to enroll in a puppy kindergarten training class, suggestions will be made as to the best collar and leash for your young puppy. I say "fortunate" because your puppy will be in a class with puppies in his age range (up to five months old) of all breeds and sizes. It's the perfect way for him to learn the right way (and the wrong way) to interact with other dogs as well as their people. You cannot teach your puppy how to interpret another dog's sign language. For a first-time puppy owner, these socialization classes are invaluable. For experienced dog owners, they are a real boon to further training.

ATTENTION

You've been using the dog's name since the minute you collected him from the breeder, so you should be able to get his attention by saying his name—with a big smile and in an excited tone of voice. His response will be the puppy equivalent of "Here I am! What are we going to do?" Your immediate response (if you haven't guessed by now) is "Good dog." Rewarding him at the moment he pays attention to you teaches him the proper way to respond when he hears his name.

EXERCISES FOR A BASIC CANINE EDUCATION

THE SIT EXERCISE

There are several ways to teach the puppy to sit. The first one is to catch him whenever he is about to sit and, as his backside nears the floor, say "Sit, good dog!" That's positive reinforcement and, if your timing is sharp, he will learn that what he's doing at that second is connected to your saying "Sit" and that you think he's clever for doing it!

Another method is to start with the puppy on his leash in front of you. Show him a treat in the palm of your right hand. Bring your hand up under his nose and, almost in slow motion, move your hand up and back so his nose goes up in the air and his head tilts back as he follows the treat in your hand. At that point, he will have to either sit or fall over, so as his back legs buckle under, say "Sit, good dog," and then give him the treat and lots of praise. You may have to begin with your hand lightly running up his chest, actually lifting his chin up until he sits. Some (usually older) dogs require gentle pressure on their hindquarters with the left hand, in which case the dog should be on your left side. Puppies

generally do not appreciate this physical dominance.

After a few times, you should be able to show the dog a treat in the open palm of your hand, raise your hand waist-high as you say "Sit" and have him sit. You thereby will have taught him two things at the same time. Both the verbal command and the motion of the hand are signals for the sit. Your puppy is watching you almost more than he is listening to you, so what you do is just as important as what you say.

Don't save any of these drills only for training sessions. Use them as much as possible at odd times during a normal day. The dog should always sit before being given his food dish. He should sit to let you go through a doorway first, when the doorbell rings or when you stop to speak to someone on the street.

THE DOWN EXERCISE
Before beginning to teach the down command, you must consider how the dog feels about this exercise. To him, "down" is a submissive position. Being flat on the floor with you standing over him is not his idea of fun. It's up to you to let him know that, while it may not be fun, the reward of your approval is worth his effort.

Start with the puppy on your left side in a sit position. Hold the leash right above his collar in your left hand. Have an extra-

Your German Pinscher may need some assistance assuming the down position until he learns that there is nothing to fear.

special treat, such as a small piece of cooked chicken or hot dog, in your right hand. Place it at the end of the pup's nose and steadily move your hand down and forward along the ground. Hold the leash to prevent a sudden lunge for the food. As the puppy goes into the down position, say "Down" very gently.

The difficulty with this exercise is twofold: it's both the submissive aspect and the fact that most people say the word "Down" as if they were drill sergeants in charge of recruits! So issue the command sweetly, give him the treat and have the pup maintain the down position for several seconds. If he tries to get up immediately, place your hands on his shoulders and press down gently, giving him a very quiet "Good dog." As you progress with this lesson, increase the "down time" until he will hold it until you say "Okay" (his cue for release). Practice this one in the house at various times throughout the day.

By increasing the length of time during which the dog must maintain the down position, you'll find many uses for it. For example, he can lie at your feet in the vet's office or anywhere that both of you have to wait, when you are on the phone, while the family is eating and so forth. If you progress to training for competitive obedience, he'll

Praise and perhaps a treat are rewards that will help your Pinscher learn that following your commands really pays off.

already be all set for the exercise called the "long down."

THE STAY EXERCISE

You can teach your German Pinscher to stay in the sit, down and stand positions. To teach the sit/stay, have the dog sit on your left side. Hold the leash at waist level in your left hand and let the dog know that you have a treat in your closed right hand. Step forward on your right foot as you say "Stay." Immediately turn and stand directly in front of the dog, keeping your right hand up high so he'll keep his eye on the treat hand and maintain the sit position for a count of five. Return to your original position and offer the reward.

Increase the length of the sit/stay each time until the dog can hold it for at least 30 seconds without moving. After about a week of success, move out on your right foot and take two steps before turning to face the dog. Give the "Stay" hand signal (left palm held up, facing the dog) as you leave. He gets the treat when you return and he holds the sit/stay. Increase the distance that you walk away from him before turning until you reach the length of your training leash. But don't rush it! Go back to the beginning if he moves before he should. No matter what the lesson, never be upset by having to back up for a few days. The repetition and practice are what will make your dog reliable in these commands. It won't do any good to move on to something more difficult if the command is not mastered at the easier levels. Above all, even if you do get frustrated, never let your puppy know! Always keep a positive, upbeat attitude during training, which will transmit to your dog for positive results.

The down/stay is taught in the same way once the dog is completely reliable and steady with the down command. Again, don't rush it. With the dog in the down position on your left side, step out on your right foot as you say "Stay." Return by walking around in back of the dog and into your original position. While you are training, it's okay to murmur something like "Hold on" to encourage him to stay put. When the dog will stay without moving when you are at a distance of 3 or 4 feet, begin to increase the length of time before you return. Be sure he holds the

down on your return until you say "Okay." At that point, he gets his treat—just so he'll remember for next time that it's not over until it's over.

THE COME EXERCISE

No command is more important to the safety of your German Pinscher than "Come." It is what you should say every single time you see the puppy running toward you: "Fritzy, come! Good dog." During playtime, run a few feet away from the puppy and turn and tell him to "Come" as he is already running to you. You can go so far as to teach your puppy two things at once if you squat down and hold out your arms. As the pup gets close to you and you're saying "Good dog," bring your right arm in about waist high. Now he's also learning the hand signal, an excellent device should you be on the phone when you need to get him to come to you! You'll also both be one step ahead when you enter obedience classes.

When the puppy responds to your well-timed "Come," try it with the puppy on the training leash. This time, catch him off guard while he's sniffing a leaf or watching a bird: "Fritzy, come!" You may have to pause for a split second after his name to be sure you have his attention. If the puppy shows any sign of confusion, give the leash a mild jerk and take a couple of steps backward. Do not repeat the command. In this case, you should say "Good come" as he reaches you.

That's the number-one rule of training. Each command word is given just once. Anything more is nagging. You'll also notice that all commands are one word only. Even when they are actually two words, you say them as one.

Never call the dog to come to you—with or without his name—if you are angry or intend to correct him for some misbehavior. When correcting the pup, you go to him. Your dog must always connect "Come" with something pleasant and with your approval; then you can rely on his response.

Puppies, like children, have notoriously short attention spans, so don't overdo it with any of the training. Keep each lesson short. Break it up with a quick run around the yard or a ball toss, repeat the lesson and quit as soon as the pup gets it right. That way, you will always end with a "Good dog."

Life isn't perfect and neither are puppies. A time will come, often around 10 months of age, when he'll become "selectively deaf" or choose to "forget" his name. He may respond by wagging his tail (and even seeming to smile at you) with a look that says "Make me!" Laugh, throw his favorite toy and skip the lesson you had planned. Pups will be pups!

The Heel Exercise

The second most important command to teach, after the

LET'S GO!

Many people use "Let's go" instead of "Heel" when teaching their dogs to behave on lead. It sounds more like fun! When beginning to teach the heel, whatever command you use, always step off on your left foot. That's the one next to the dog, who is on your left side, in case you've forgotten. Keep a loose leash. When the dog pulls ahead, stop, bring him back and begin again. Use treats to guide him around turns.

come, is the heel. When you are walking your growing puppy, you need to be in control. Besides, it looks terrible to be pulled and yanked down the street, and it's not much fun either. Your eight-to ten-week-old puppy will probably follow you everywhere, but that's his natural instinct, not your control over the situation. However, any time he does follow you, you can say "Heel" and be ahead of the game, as he will learn to associate this command with the action of following you before you even begin teaching him to heel.

There is a very precise, almost military, procedure for teaching your dog to heel. As with all other obedience training, begin with the dog on your left side. He will be in a very nice sit and you will have the training leash across your chest. Hold the loop and folded leash in your right hand. Pick up the slack leash above the dog in your left hand and hold it loosely at your side. Step out on your left foot as you say "Heel." If the puppy does not move, give a gentle tug or pat your left leg to get him started. If he surges ahead of you, stop and pull him back gently until he is at your side. Tell him to sit and begin again.

Walk a few steps and stop while the puppy is correctly beside you. Tell him to sit and give mild verbal praise. (More enthusiastic praise will encourage him to think the lesson is over.) Repeat the lesson, increasing the number of steps you take only as long as the dog is heeling nicely beside you. When you end the lesson, have him hold the sit, then give him the "Okay" to let him know that this is the end of the lesson. Praise him so that he knows he did a good job.

The cure for excessive pulling (a common problem) is to stop when the dog is no more than 2 or 3 feet ahead of you. Guide him back into position and begin again. With a really determined puller, try switching to a head collar. When used properly, this will automatically turn the pup's head toward you so you can bring him back easily to the heel position. Give quiet, reassuring praise every time the leash goes slack and he's staying with you.

Staying and heeling can take a lot out of a dog, so provide

Posing in front of an agility tunnel, this pup bred by Betsy Spilis has the potential for a bright future in a multitude of pursuits.

playtime and free-running exercise to shake off the stress when the lessons are over. You don't want him to associate training with all work and no fun.

OBEDIENCE CLASSES

The advantages of an obedience class are that your dog will have to learn amid the distractions of other people and dogs and that your mistakes will be quickly corrected by the trainer. Teaching your dog along with a qualified instructor and other handlers who may have more dog experience than you is another plus of the class environment. The instructor and other handlers can help you to find the most efficient way of teaching your dog a command or exercise. It's often easier to learn by other people's mistakes than your own. You will also learn all of the requirements for competitive obedience trials, in which you can earn titles and go on to advanced jumping and retrieving exercises, which are fun for many dogs. Obedience classes build the foundation needed for many other canine activities.

TRAINING FOR OTHER ACTIVITIES

Once your dog has basic obedience under his collar and is 12 months of age, you can enter the world of agility training. Dogs think agility is pure fun, like being turned loose in an amusement park full of

obstacles! In addition to agility, there is tracking, which is open to all "nosey" dogs (which would include all dogs!). For those who like to volunteer, there is the wonderful feeling of owning a therapy dog and visiting hospices, nursing homes and veterans' homes to bring smiles, comfort and companionship to those who live there.

Around the house, your German Pinscher can be taught to do some simple chores. You might teach him to carry small household items or to fetch the morning newspaper. The kids can teach the dog all kinds of tricks, from playing hide-and-seek to balancing a biscuit on his nose. A family dog is what rounds out the family. Everything he does, including sitting in your lap and gazing lovingly at you, represents the bonus of owning a dog.

Not many German Pinschers are avid fans of water sports, but if your pup is the exception make sure he is properly equipped for safety.

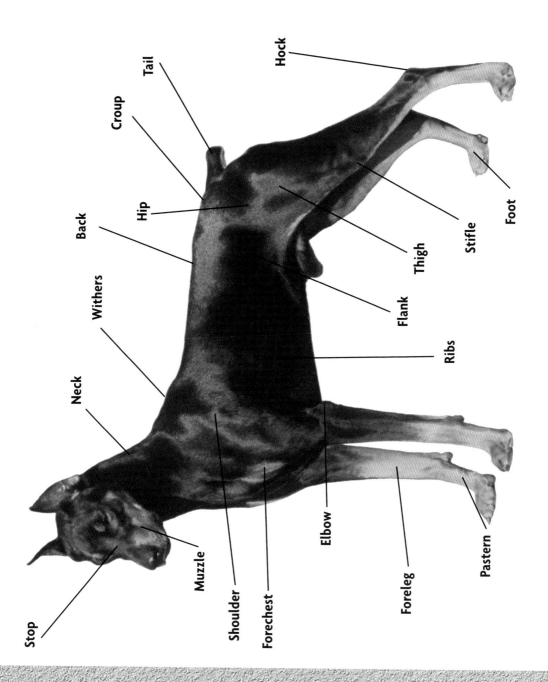

Hock

Tail

Croup

Hip

Back

Withers

Neck

Muzzle

Stop

Shoulder

Forechest

Elbow

Foreleg

Pastern

Ribs

Flank

Thigh

Stifle

Foot

PHYSICAL STRUCTURE OF THE GERMAN PINSCHER

HEALTHCARE OF YOUR

GERMAN PINSCHER

By Lowell Ackerman DVM, DACVD

HEALTHCARE FOR A LIFETIME

When you own a dog, you become his healthcare advocate over his entire lifespan, as well as being the one to shoulder the financial burden of such care. Accordingly, it is worthwhile to focus on prevention rather than treatment, as you and your pet will both be happier.

Of course, the best place to have begun your program of preventive healthcare is with the initial purchase or adoption of your dog. There is no way of guaranteeing that your new furry friend is free of medical problems, but there are some things you can do to improve your odds. You certainly should have done adequate research into the German Pinscher and have selected your puppy carefully rather than buying on impulse. Health issues aside, a large number of pet abandonment and relinquishment cases arise from a mismatch between pet needs and owner expectations. This is entirely preventable with appropriate planning and finding a good breeder.

Regarding healthcare issues specifically, it is very difficult to make blanket statements about where to acquire a problem-free pet, but, again, a reputable breeder is your best bet. In an ideal situation you have the opportunity to see both parents, get references from other owners of the breeder's pups and see genetic-testing documentation for several generations of the litter's ancestors. At the very least, you must thoroughly investigate the German Pinscher and the problems inherent in that breed, as well as the genetic testing available to screen for those problems. Genetic testing offers some important benefits, but testing is available for only a few disorders in a relatively small number of breeds and is not available for some of the most common genetic diseases, such as hip dysplasia, cataracts, epilepsy, cardiomyopathy, etc. This area of research is indeed exciting and increasingly important, and advances will continue to be made each year. In fact, recent research has shown that there is

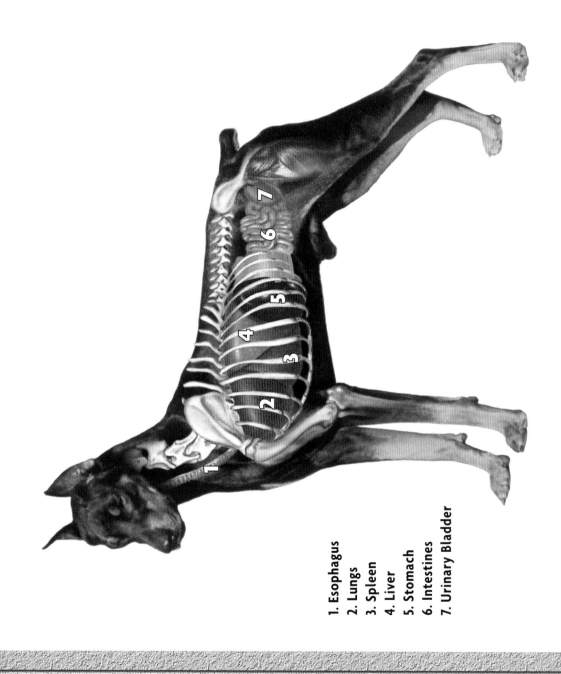

1. Esophagus
2. Lungs
3. Spleen
4. Liver
5. Stomach
6. Intestines
7. Urinary Bladder

INTERNAL ORGANS OF THE GERMAN PINSCHER

an equivalent dog gene for 75% of known human genes, so research done in either species is likely to benefit the other.

We've also discussed that evaluating the behavioral nature of your German Pinscher and that of his immediate family members is an important part of the selection process that cannot be underestimated or overemphasized. It is sometimes difficult to evaluate temperament in puppies because certain behavioral tendencies, such as some forms of aggression, may not be immediately evident. More dogs are euthanized each year for behavioral reasons than for all medical conditions combined, so it is critical to take temperament issues seriously. Start with a well-balanced, friendly companion and put the time and effort into proper socialization, and you will both be rewarded with a fulfilling relationship for the life of the dog.

Assuming that you have started off with a pup from healthy, sound stock, you then become responsible for helping your veterinarian keep your pet healthy. Some crucial things happen before you even bring your puppy home. Parasite control typically begins at two weeks of age, and vaccinations typically begin at six to eight weeks of age. A pre-pubertal evaluation is typically scheduled for about six months of age. At this time, a dental evaluation is done (since the adult teeth are now in), heartworm prevention is started and neutering or spaying is most commonly done.

It is critical to commence regular dental care at home if you have not already done so. It may not sound very important, but most dogs have active periodontal disease by four years of age if they don't have their teeth cleaned regularly at home, not just at their veterinary exams. Dental problems lead to more than just bad "doggy breath"— gum disease can have very serious medical consequences. If you start brushing your dog's teeth and using antiseptic rinses from a young age, your dog will be accustomed to it and will not resist. The results will be healthy dentition, which your pet will need to enjoy a long, healthy life.

Most dogs are considered adults at a year of age; the German Pinscher continues filling out for about another year. Even individual dogs within each breed have different healthcare requirements, so work with your veterinarian to determine what will be needed and what your role should be. This doctor-client relationship is important, because as vaccination guidelines change, there may not be an annual "vaccine visit" scheduled. You must make sure that you see your

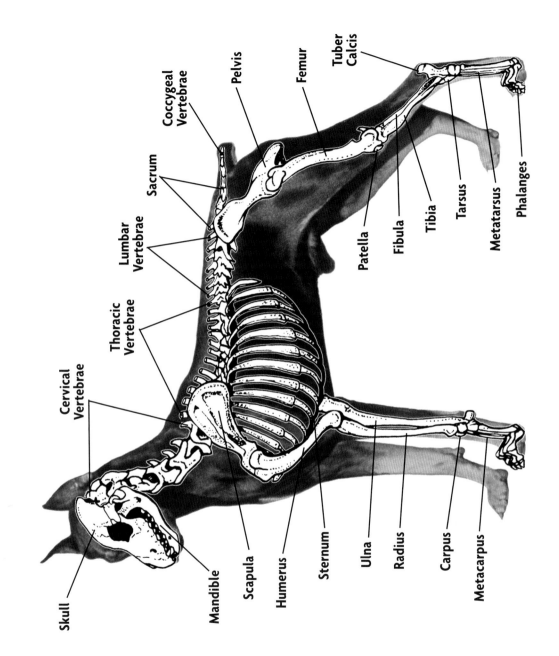

Coccygeal
Vertebrae

Pelvis

Femur

Tuber
Calcis

Sacrum

Lumbar
Vertebrae

Patella

Fibula

Tibia

Tarsus

Metatarsus

Phalanges

Thoracic
Vertebrae

Cervical
Vertebrae

Skull

Mandible

Scapula

Humerus

Sternum

Ulna

Radius

Carpus

Metacarpus

SKELETAL STRUCTURE OF THE GERMAN PINSCHER

veterinarian at least annually, even if no vaccines are due, because this is the best opportunity to coordinate healthcare activities and to make sure that no medical issues creep by unaddressed.

When your German Pinscher reaches three-quarters of his anticipated lifespan or as the vet determines, he is considered a "senior" and likely requires some special care. In general, if you've been taking great care of your canine companion throughout his formative and adult years, the transition to senior status should be a smooth one. Age is not a disease, and as long as everything is functioning as it should, there is no reason why most of late adulthood should not be rewarding for both you and your pet. This is especially true if you have tended to the details, such as regular veterinary visits, proper dental care, excellent nutrition and management of bone and joint issues.

At this stage in your German Pinscher's life, your veterinarian may want to schedule visits twice yearly, instead of once, to run some laboratory screenings, electrocardiograms and the like, and to change the diet to something more digestible. Catching problems early is the best way to manage them effectively. Treating the early stages of heart disease is so much easier than trying to intervene

when there is more significant damage to the heart muscle. Similarly, managing the beginning of kidney problems is fairly routine if there is no significant kidney damage. Other problems, like cognitive dysfunction (similar to senility and Alzheimer's disease), cancer, diabetes and arthritis, are more common in older dogs, but all can be treated to help the dog live as many happy, comfortable years as possible. Just as in people, medical management is more effective (and less expensive) when you catch things early.

SELECTING A VETERINARIAN

There is probably no more important decision that you will make regarding your pet's healthcare than the selection of his doctor. Your pet's veterinarian will be a pediatrician, family-practice physician and gerontologist, depending on the dog's life stage, and will be the individual who makes recommendations regarding issues such as when specialists need to be consulted, when diagnostic testing and/or therapeutic intervention is needed and when you will need to seek outside emergency and critical-care services. Your vet will act as your advocate and liaison throughout these processes.

Everyone has his own idea about what to look for in a vet, an individual who will play a big role in his dog's (and, of course, his own) life for many years to come. For some, it is the compassionate caregiver with whom they hope to develop a professional relationship to span the lives of their dogs and even their future pets. For others, they are seeking a clinician with keen diagnostic and therapeutic insight who can deliver state-of-the-art healthcare. Still others need a veterinary facility that is open evenings and weekends, is in close proximity or provides mobile veterinary services to accommodate their schedules; these people may not much mind that their dogs might see different veterinarians on each visit. Just as we have different reasons for selecting our own healthcare professionals (e.g.,

Your German Pinscher relies on you for good healthcare. When properly maintained, he will retain his lively exuberance throughout his life.

covered by insurance plan, expert in field, convenient location, etc.), we should not expect that there is a one-size-fits-all recommendation for selecting a veterinarian and veterinary practice. The best advice is to be honest in your assessment of what you expect from a veterinary practice and to conscientiously research the options in your area. You will quickly appreciate that not all veterinary practices are the same, and you will be happiest with one that truly meets your needs.

There is another point to be considered in the selection of veterinary services. Not that long ago, a single veterinarian would attempt to manage all medical and surgical issues as they arose. That was often problematic, because veterinarians are trained in many species and many diseases, and it was just impossible for general veterinary practitioners to be experts in every species, every field and every ailment. However, just as in the human healthcare fields, specialization has allowed general practitioners to concentrate on primary healthcare delivery, especially wellness and the prevention of infectious diseases, and to utilize a network of specialists to assist in the management of conditions that require specific expertise and experience. Thus there are now many types of veterinary specialists, including dermatologists, cardiologists, ophthalmologists, surgeons, internists, oncologists, neurologists, behaviorists, criticalists and others to help primary-care veterinarians deal with complicated medical challenges. In most cases, specialists see cases referred by primary-care veterinarians, make diagnoses and set up management plans. From there, the animals' ongoing care is returned to their primary-care veterinarians. This important team approach to your pet's medical-care needs has provided opportunities for advanced care and an unparalleled level of quality to be delivered.

With all of the opportunities for your German Pinscher to receive high-quality veterinary medical care, there is another topic that needs to be addressed at the same time—cost. It's been said that you can have excellent healthcare or inexpensive healthcare, but never both; this is as true in veterinary medicine as it is in human medicine. While veterinary costs are a fraction of what the same services cost in the human healthcare arena, it is still difficult to deal with unanticipated medical costs, especially since they can easily creep into hundreds or even thousands of dollars if specialists or emergency services become

INSURANCE
Pet insurance policies are very cost-effective (and very inexpensive by human health-insurance standards), but make sure that you buy the policy long before you intend to use it (preferably starting in puppyhood, because coverage will exclude pre-existing conditions) and that you are actually buying an indemnity insurance plan from an insurance company that is regulated by your state or province. Many insurance policy look-alikes are actually discount clubs that are redeemable only at specific locations and for specific services. An indemnity plan covers your pet at almost all veterinary, specialty and emergency practices and is an excellent way to manage your pet's ongoing healthcare needs.

involved. However, there are ways of managing these risks. The easiest is to buy pet health insurance and realize that its foremost purpose is not to cover routine healthcare visits but rather to serve as an umbrella for those rainy days when your pet needs medical care and you don't want to worry about whether or not you can afford that care.

VACCINATIONS AND INFECTIOUS DISEASES
There has never been an easier time to prevent a variety of

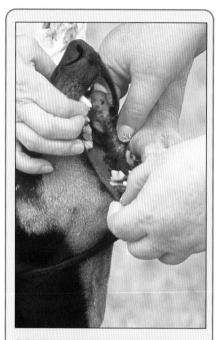

DENTAL WARNING SIGNS

A veterinary dental exam is necessary if you notice one or any combination of the following in your dog:

• Broken, loose or missing teeth;
• Loss of appetite (which could be due to mouth pain or illness caused by infection);
• Gum abnormalities, including redness, swelling and bleeding;
• Drooling, with or without blood;
• Yellowing of the teeth or gumline, indicating tartar;
• Bad breath.

infectious diseases in your dog, but the advances we've made in veterinary medicine come with a price—choice. Now while it may seem that choice is a good thing (and it is), it has never been more difficult for the pet owner (or the veterinarian) to make an informed decision about the best way to protect pets through vaccination.

Years ago, it was just accepted that puppies got a starter series of vaccinations and then annual "boosters" throughout their lives to keep them protected. As more and more vaccines became available, consumers wanted the convenience of having all of that protection in a single injection. The result was "multivalent" vaccines that crammed a lot of protection into a single syringe. The manufacturers' recommendations were to give the vaccines annually, and this was a simple enough protocol to follow. However, as veterinary medicine has become more sophisticated and we have started looking more at healthcare quandaries rather than convenience, it became necessary to reevaluate the situation and deal with some tough questions. It is important to realize that whether or not to use a particular vaccine depends on the risk of contracting the disease against which it protects, the severity of the disease if it is contracted, the duration of immunity provided by the vaccine, the safety of the product and the needs of the individual animal. In a very general sense, rabies, distemper, hepatitis and parvovirus are considered core vaccine needs, while parainfluenza, *Bordetella bronchiseptica*, leptospirosis, coronavirus and borreliosis (Lyme disease) are considered non-core needs and best reserved for animals that demonstrate reasonable risk of contracting the diseases.

NEUTERING/SPAYING

Sterilization procedures (neutering for males/spaying for females) are meant to accomplish several purposes. While the underlying premise is to address the risk of pet overpopulation, there are also some medical and behavioral benefits to the surgeries. For females, spaying prior to the first estrus (heat cycle) leads to a marked reduction in the risk of mammary cancer and other serious female problems. There also will be no manifestations of "heat" to attract male dogs and no bleeding in the house. For males, there is prevention of testicular cancer and a reduction in the risk of prostate problems. In both sexes there may be some limited reduction in aggressive behaviors toward other dogs, and some diminishing of urine marking, roaming and mounting.

While neutering and spaying do indeed prevent animals from contributing to pet overpopulation, even no-cost and low-cost neutering options have not eliminated the problem. Perhaps one of the main reasons for this is that individuals that intentionally breed their dogs and those that allow their animals to run at large are the main causes of unwanted offspring. Also, animals in shelters are often there because they were abandoned or relinquished, not because they came from unplanned matings. Neutering/spaying is important, but it should be considered in the context of the real causes of animals' ending up in shelters and eventually being euthanized.

One of the important considerations regarding neutering is that it is a surgical procedure. This sometimes gets lost in discussions of low-cost procedures and commoditization of the process. In females, spaying is specifically referred to as an ovariohysterectomy. In this procedure, a midline incision is made in the abdomen and the entire uterus and both ovaries are surgically removed. While this is

Every puppy should be vaccinated. The vaccinations are started with the breeder and continued by your dog's veterinarian.

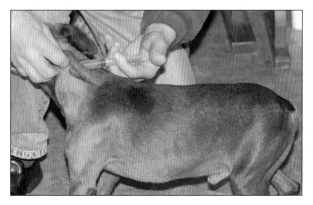

a major invasive surgical procedure, it usually has few complications, because it is typically performed on healthy young animals. However, it is major surgery, as any woman who has had a hysterectomy will attest.

In males, neutering has traditionally referred to castration, which involves the surgical removal of both testicles. While still a significant piece of surgery, there is not the abdominal exposure that is required in the female surgery. In addition, there is now a chemical sterilization option, in which a solution is injected into each testicle, leading to atrophy of the sperm-producing cells. This can typically be done under sedation rather than full anesthesia. This is a relatively new approach, and there are no long-term clinical studies yet available.

Neutering/spaying is typically done around six months of age at most veterinary hospitals, although techniques have been pioneered to perform the procedures in animals as young as eight weeks of age. In general, the surgeries on the very young animals are done for the specific reason of sterilizing them before they go to their new homes. This is done in some shelter hospitals for assurance that the animals will definitely not produce any pups. Otherwise, these organizations need to rely on owners to comply with their wishes to have the animals "altered" at a later date, something that does not always happen.

There are some exciting immunocontraceptive "vaccines" currently under development, and there may be a time when contraception in pets will not require surgical procedures. We anxiously await these developments.

TAKING YOUR DOG'S TEMPERATURE

It is important to know how to take your dog's temperature at times when you think he may be ill. It's not the most enjoyable task, but it can be done without too much difficulty. It's easier with a helper, preferably someone with whom the dog is friendly, so that one of you can hold the dog while the other inserts the thermometer.

Before inserting the thermometer, coat the end with petroleum jelly. Insert the thermometer slowly and gently into the dog's rectum about one inch. Wait for the reading, about two minutes. Be sure to remove the thermometer carefully and clean it thoroughly after each use.

A dog's normal body temperature is between 100.5 and 102.5 degrees F. Immediate veterinary attention is required if the dog's temperature is below 99 or above 104 degrees F.

COMMON INFECTIOUS DISEASES

Let's discuss some of the diseases that create the need for vaccination in the first place. Following are the major canine infectious diseases and a simple explanation of each.

Rabies: A devastating viral disease that can be fatal in dogs and people. In fact, vaccination of dogs and cats is an important public-health measure to create a resistant animal buffer population to protect people from contracting the disease. Vaccination schedules are determined on a government level and are not optional for pet owners; rabies vaccination is required by law in all 50 states.

Parvovirus: A severe, potentially life-threatening disease that is easily transmitted between dogs. There are four strains of the virus, but it is believed that there is significant "cross-protection" between strains that may be included in individual vaccines.

Distemper: A potentially severe and life-threatening disease with a relatively high risk of exposure, especially in certain regions. In very high-risk distemper environments, young pups may be vaccinated with human measles vaccine, a related virus that offers cross-protection when administered at four to ten weeks of age.

Hepatitis: Caused by canine adenovirus type 1 (CAV-1), but since vaccination with the causative virus has a higher rate of adverse effects, cross-protection is derived from the use of adenovirus type 2 (CAV-2), a cause of respiratory disease and one of the potential causes of canine cough. Vaccination with CAV-2 provides long-term immunity against hepatitis, but relatively less protection against respiratory infection.

Canine cough: Also called tracheobronchitis, actually a fairly complicated result of viral and bacterial offenders; therefore, even with vaccination, protection is incomplete. Wherever dogs congregate, canine cough will likely be spread among them. Intranasal vaccination with *Bordetella* and parainfluenza is the best safeguard, but the duration of immunity does not appear to be very long, typically a year at most. These are non-core vaccines, but vaccination is sometimes mandated by boarding kennels, obedience classes, dog shows and other places where dogs congregate to try to minimize spread of infection.

Leptospirosis: A potentially fatal disease that is more common in some geographic regions. It is capable of being spread to humans. The disease varies with the individual "serovar," or strain, of *Leptospira* involved. Since there does not appear to be much cross-protection between serovars, protection is only as good as the likelihood that the serovar in the vaccine is the same as the one in the pet's local environment. Problems with *Leptospira* vaccines are that protection does not last very long, side effects are not uncommon and a large percentage of dogs (perhaps 30%) may not respond to vaccination.

Borrelia burgdorferi: The cause of Lyme disease, the risk of which varies with the geographic area in which the pet lives and travels. Lyme disease is spread by deer ticks in the eastern US and western black-legged ticks in the western part of the country, and the risk of exposure is high in some regions. Lameness, fever and inappetence are most commonly seen in affected dogs. The extent of protection from the vaccine has not been conclusively demonstrated.

Coronavirus: This disease has a high risk of exposure, especially in areas where dogs congregate, but it typically causes only mild to moderate digestive upset (diarrhea, vomiting, etc.). Vaccines are available, but the duration of protection is believed to be relatively short and the effectiveness of the vaccine in preventing infection is considered low.

There are many other vaccinations available, including those for *Giardia* and canine adenovirus-1. While there may be some specific indications for their use, and local risk factors to be considered, they are not widely recommended for most dogs.

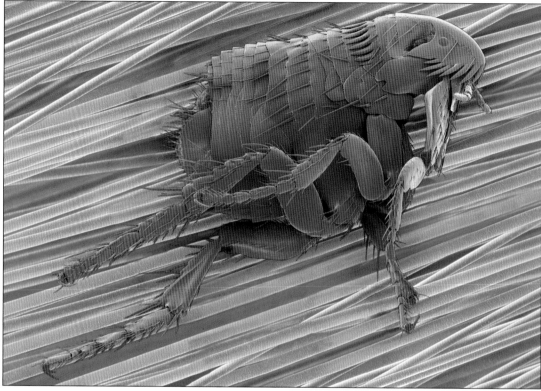

A scanning electron micrograph of a dog flea, Ctenocephalides canis, on dog hair.

EXTERNAL PARASITES

FLEAS

Fleas have been around for millions of years and, while we have better tools now for controlling them than at any time in the past, there still is little chance that they will end up on an endangered species list. Actually, they are very well adapted to living on our pets, and they continue to adapt as we make advances.

The female flea can consume 15 times her weight in blood during active reproduction and can lay as many as 40 eggs a day. These eggs are very resistant to the effects of insecticides. They hatch into larvae, which then mature and spin cocoons. The immature fleas reside in this pupal stage until the time is right for feeding. This pupal stage is also very resistant to the effects of insecticides, and pupae can last in the environment without feeding for many months. Newly emergent fleas are attracted to animals by the warmth of the animals' bodies, movement and exhaled carbon dioxide. However, when they first emerge from their cocoons, they orient towards light; thus when an animal passes between a flea and the light source, casting a shadow, the flea pounces and starts to feed. If the animal turns out to be a dog or cat, the reproductive cycle continues. If the flea lands on another type of animal, including a person, the flea will bite but will then look for a more appropriate host. An emerging adult flea can survive without feeding for up to 12 months but, once it tastes blood, it can survive off its host for only 3 to 4 days.

It was once thought that fleas spend most of their lives in the environment, but we now know that fleas won't willingly jump off a dog unless leaping to another dog or when physically removed by brushing, bathing or other manipu-lation. Flea eggs, on the other hand, are shiny and smooth, and they roll off the animal and into the environ-ment. The eggs, larvae and pupae then exist in the environment, but once the adult finds a susceptible animal, it's home sweet home until the flea is forced to seek refuge elsewhere.

Since adult fleas live on the animal and immature forms survive in the environment, a successful treatment plan must address all stages of the flea life cycle. There are now several safe and effective flea-control products that can be applied on a monthly

FLEA PREVENTION FOR YOUR DOG

- Discuss with your veterinarian the safest product to protect your dog, likely in the form of a monthly tablet or a liquid preparation placed on the back of the dog's neck.
- For dogs suffering from flea-bite dermatitis, a shampoo or topical insecticide treatment is required.
- Your lawn and property should be sprayed with an insecticide designed to kill fleas and ticks that lurk outdoors.
- Using a flea comb, check the dog's coat regularly for any signs of parasites.
- Practice good housekeeping. Vacuum floors, carpets and furniture regularly, especially in the areas that the dog frequents, and wash the dog's bedding weekly.
- Follow up house-cleaning with carpet shampoos and sprays to rid the house of fleas at all stages of development. Insect growth regulators are the safest option.

basis. These include fipronil, imidacloprid, selamectin and permethrin (found in several formulations). Most of these products have significant flea-killing rates within 24 hours. However, none of them will control the immature forms in the environment. To accomplish this, there are a variety of insect growth regulators that can be

THE FLEA'S LIFE CYCLE

What came first, the flea or the egg? This age-old mystery is more difficult to comprehend than the actual cycle of the flea. Fleas usually live only about four months. A female can lay 2,000 eggs in her lifetime.

Egg

PHOTO BY CAROLINA BIOLOGICAL SUPPLY CO.

After ten days of rolling around your carpet or under your furniture, the eggs hatch into larvae, which feed on various and sundry debris. In days or months, depending on the climate, the larvae spin cocoons and develop into the pupal or nymph stage, which quickly develop into fleas.

Larva

PHOTO BY CAROLINA BIOLOGICAL SUPPLY CO.

Pupa

These immature fleas must locate a host within 10 to 14 days or they will die. Only about 1% of the flea population exist as adult fleas, while the other 99% exist as eggs, larvae or pupae.

Adult

KILL FLEAS THE NATURAL WAY

If you choose not to go the route of conventional medication, there are some natural ways to ward off fleas:

• Dust your dog with a natural flea powder, composed of such herbal goodies as rosemary, wormwood, pennyroyal, citronella, rue, tobacco powder and eucalyptus.

• Apply diatomaceous earth, the fossilized remains of single-cell algae, to your carpets, furniture and pet's bedding. Even though it's not good for dogs, it's even worse for fleas, which will dry up swiftly and die.

• Brush your dog frequently, give him adequate exercise and let him fast occasionally. All of these activities strengthen the dog's immune system and make him more resistant to disease and parasites.

• Bathe your dog with a capful of pennyroyal or eucalyptus oil.

• Feed a natural diet, free of additives and preservatives. Add a little fresh garlic and brewer's yeast to the dog's morning portion, as these items have flea-repelling properties.

sprayed into the environment (e.g., pyriproxyfen, methoprene, fenoxycarb) as well as insect development inhibitors such as lufenuron that can be administered. These compounds have no effect on adult fleas, but they stop immature forms from developing into adults. In years gone by, we relied heavily on toxic insecticides (such as organophosphates, organochlorines and carbamates) to manage the flea problem, but today's options are not only much safer to use on our pets but also safer for the environment.

Ticks

Ticks are members of the spider class (arachnids) and are blood-sucking parasites capable of transmitting a variety of diseases, including Lyme disease, ehrlichiosis, babesiosis and Rocky Mountain spotted fever. It's easy to see ticks on your own skin, but it is more of a challenge when your German Pinscher is affected. Whenever you happen to be planning a stroll in a tick-infested area (especially forests, grassy or wooded areas or parks) be prepared to do a thorough inspection of your dog afterward to search for ticks. Ticks can be tricky, so make sure you spend time looking in the ears, between the toes and everywhere else where a tick might hide. Ticks need to be attached for 24–72 hours before they transmit most of the diseases that they carry, so you do have a window of opportunity for some preventive intervention.

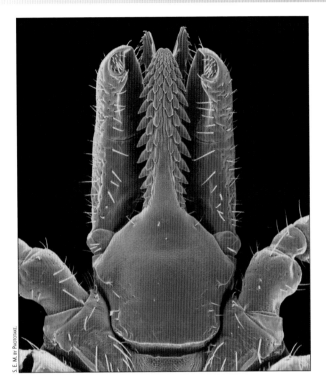

S. E. M. BY PHOTOTAKE.

A scanning electron micrograph of the head of a female deer tick, *Ixodes dammini,* a parasitic tick that carries Lyme disease.

A TICKING BOMB

There is nothing good about a tick's harpooning his nose into your dog's skin. Among the diseases caused by ticks are Rocky Mountain spotted fever, canine ehrlichiosis, canine babesiosis, canine hepatozoonosis and Lyme disease. If a dog is allergic to the saliva of a female wood tick, he can develop tick paralysis.

Female ticks live to eat and breed. They can lay between 4,000 and 5,000 eggs and they die soon after. Males, on the other hand, live only to mate with the females and continue the process as long as they are able. Most ticks live on multiple hosts before parasitizing dogs. The immature forms typically reside on grass and shrubs, waiting for suscep-tible animals to walk by. The larvae and nymph stages typically feed on wildlife.

If only a few ticks are present on a dog, they can be plucked out, but it is important to remove the entire head and mouthparts,

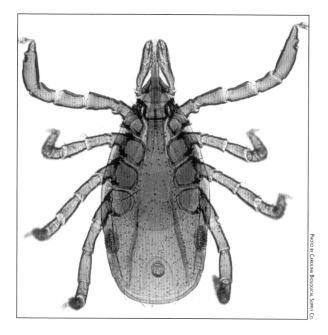

Photo by Carolina Biological Supply Co.

**Deer tick,
*Ixodes dammini.***

disposed of in a container of alcohol or household bleach.

Some of the newer flea products, specifically those with fipronil, selamectin and permethrin, have effect against some, but not all, species of tick. Flea collars containing appropriate pesticides (e.g., propoxur, chlorfen-vinphos) can aid in tick control. In most areas, such collars should be placed on animals in March, at the beginning of the tick season, and changed regularly. Leaving the collar on when the pesticide level is waning invites the development of resistance. Amitraz collars are also good for tick control, and the active ingredient does not interfere with other flea-control products. The ingredient helps prevent the attachment of ticks to the skin and will cause those ticks already on the skin to detach themselves.

which may be deeply embedded in the skin. This is best accomplished with forceps designed especially for this purpose; fingers can be used but should be protected with rubber gloves, plastic wrap or at least a paper towel. The tick should be grasped as closely as possible to the animal's skin and should be pulled upward with steady, even pressure. Do not squeeze, crush or puncture the body of the tick or you risk exposure to any disease carried by that tick. Once the ticks have been removed, the sites of attachment should be disinfected. Your hands should then be washed with soap and water to further minimize risk of contagion. The tick should be

TICK CONTROL
Removal of underbrush and leaf litter and the thinning of trees in areas where tick control is desired are recom-mended. These actions remove the cover and food sources for small animals that serve as hosts for ticks. With continued mowing of grasses in these areas, the probability of ticks' surviving is further reduced. A variety of insecticide ingredients (e.g., resmethrin, carbaryl, permethrin, chlorpyrifos, dioxathion and allethrin) are registered for tick control around the home.

MITES

Mites are tiny arachnid parasites that parasitize the skin of dogs. Skin diseases caused by mites are referred to as "mange," and there are many different forms seen in dogs. These forms are very different from one another, each one warranting an individual description.

Sarcoptic mange, or scabies, is one of the itchiest conditions that affects dogs. The microscopic *Sarcoptes* mites burrow into the superficial layers of the skin and can drive dogs crazy with itchiness. They are also communicable to people, although they can't complete their reproductive cycle on people. In addition to being tiny, the mites also are often difficult to find when trying to make a diagnosis. Skin scrapings from multiple areas are examined microscopically but, even then, sometimes the mites cannot be found.

Fortunately, scabies is relatively easy to treat, and there are a variety of products that will successfully kill the mites. Since the mites can't live in the environment for very long without feeding, a complete cure is usually possible within four to eight weeks.

Cheyletiellosis is caused by a relatively large mite, which sometimes can be seen even without a microscope. Often referred to as "walking dandruff," this also causes itching, but not usually as profound as with scabies.

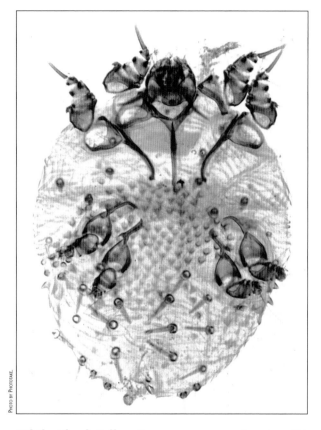

PHOTO BY PHOTOTAKE.

Sarcoptes scabiei, commonly known as the "itch mite."

While *Cheyletiella* mites can survive somewhat longer in the environment than scabies mites, they too are relatively easy to treat, being responsive to not only the medications used to treat scabies but also often to flea-control products.

Otodectes cynotis is the canine ear mite and is one of the more common causes of mange, especially in young dogs in shelters or pet stores. That's because the mites are typically present in large numbers and are quickly spread to

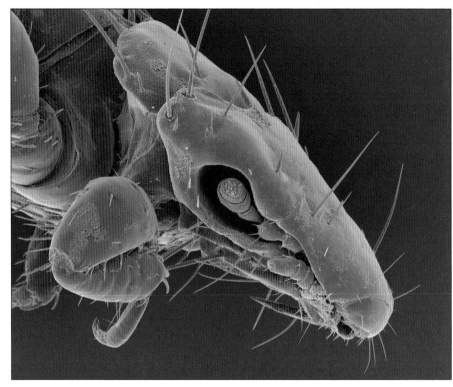

Micrograph of a dog louse, *Heterodoxus spiniger*. Female lice attach their eggs to the hairs of the dog. As the eggs hatch, the larval lice bite and feed on the blood. Lice can also feed on dead skin and hair. This feeding activity can cause hair loss and skin problems.

S. E. M. by Dr. Dennis Kunkel, University of Hawaii

nearby animals. The mites rarely do much harm but can be difficult to eradicate if the treatment regimen is not comprehensive. While many try to treat the condition with ear drops only, this is the most common cause of treatment failure. Ear drops cause the mites to simply move out of the ears and as far away as possible (usually to the base of the tail) until the insecticide levels in the ears drop to an acceptable level—then it's back to business as usual! The successful treatment of ear mites requires treating all animals in the household with a systemic insecticide, such as selamectin, or a combination of miticidal ear drops combined with whole-body flea-control preparations.

Demodicosis, sometimes referred to as red mange, can be one of the most difficult forms of mange to treat. Part of the problem has to do with the fact that the mites live in the hair follicles and they are relatively well shielded from topical and systemic products. The main issue, however, is that demodectic mange typically results only when there is some underlying process interfering with the dog's immune system.

Since *Demodex* mites are

normal residents of the skin of mammals, including humans, there is usually a mite population explosion only when the immune system fails to keep the number of mites in check. In young animals, the immune deficit may be transient or may reflect an actual inherited immune problem. In older animals, demodicosis is usually seen only when there is another disease hampering the immune system, such as diabetes, cancer, thyroid problems or the use of immune-suppressing drugs. Accordingly, treatment involves not only trying to kill the mange mites but also discerning what is interfering with immune function and correcting it if possible.

Chiggers represent several different species of mite that don't parasitize dogs specifically, but do latch on to passersby and can cause irritation. The problem is most prevalent in wooded areas in the late summer and fall. Treatment is not difficult, as the mites do not complete their life cycle on dogs and are susceptible to a variety of miticidal products.

ILLUSTRATION BY PHOTOTAKE

MOSQUITOES

Mosquitoes have long been known to transmit a variety of diseases to people, as well as just being biting pests during warm weather. They also pose a real risk to pets. Not only do they carry deadly heartworms but recently there also has been much concern over their involvement with West Nile virus. While we can avoid heartworm with the use of preventive medications, there are no such preventives for West Nile virus. The only method of prevention in endemic areas is active mosquito control. Fortunately, most dogs that have been exposed to the virus only developed flu-like symptoms and, to date, there have not been the large number of reported deaths in canines as seen in some other species.

Illustration of *Demodex folliculoram*.

MOSQUITO REPELLENT

Low concentrations of DEET (less than 10%), found in many human mosquito repellents, have been safely used in dogs but, in these concentrations, probably give only about two hours of protection. DEET may be safe in these small concentrations, but since it is not licensed for use on dogs, there is no research proving its safety for dogs. Products containing permethrin give the longest-lasting protection, perhaps two to four weeks. As DEET is not licensed for use on dogs, and both DEET and permethrin can be quite toxic to cats, appropriate care should be exercised. Other products, such as those containing oil of citronella, also have some mosquito-repellent activity, but typically have a relatively short duration of action.

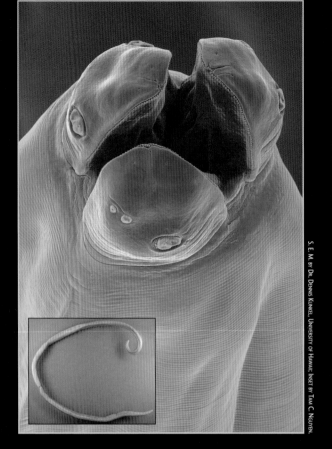

S. E. M. BY DR. DENNIS KUNKEL, UNIVERSITY OF HAWAII; INSET BY TAM C. NGUYEN.

ASCARID DANGERS

The most commonly encountered worms in dogs are roundworms known as ascarids. *Toxascaris leonine* and *Toxocara canis* are the two species that infect dogs. Subsisting in the dog's stomach and intestines, adult roundworms can grow to 7 inches in length and adult females can lay in excess of 200,000 eggs in a single day.

In humans, visceral larval migrans affects people who have ingested eggs of *Toxocara canis*, which frequently contaminates children's sandboxes, beaches and park grounds. The roundworms reside in the human's stomach and intestines, as they would in a dog's, but do not mature. Instead, they find their way to the liver, lungs and skin, or even to the heart or kidneys in severe cases. Deworming puppies is critical in preventing the infection in humans, and young children should never handle nursing pups who have not been dewormed.

The ascarid roundworm *Toxocara canis*, showing the mouth with three lips. INSET: Photomicrograph of the roundworm *Ascaris lumbricoides.*

INTERNAL PARASITES: WORMS

ASCARIDS

Ascarids are intestinal roundworms that rarely cause severe disease in dogs. Nonetheless, they are of major public health significance because they can be transferred to people. Sadly, it is children who are most commonly affected by the parasite, probably from inadvertently ingesting ascarid-contaminated soil. In fact, many yards and children's sandboxes contain appreciable numbers of ascarid eggs. So, while ascarids don't bite dogs or latch onto their intestines to suck blood, they do cause some nasty medical conditions in children and are best eradicated from our furry friends. Because pups can start passing ascarid eggs by three weeks of age, most parasite-control programs begin at two weeks of age and are repeated every two weeks until pups are eight weeks old. It is important to

HOOKED ON ANCYLOSTOMA

Adult dogs can become infected by the bloodsucking nematodes we commonly call hookworms via ingesting larvae from the ground or via the larvae penetrating the dog's skin. It is not uncommon for infected dogs to show no symptoms of hookworm infestation. Sometimes symptoms occur within ten days of exposure. These symptoms can include bloody diarrhea, anemia, loss of weight and general weakness. Dogs pass the hookworm eggs in their stools, which serves as the vet's method of identifying the infestation. The hookworm larvae can encyst themselves in the dog's tissues and be released when the dog is experiencing stress.

Caused by an *Ancylostoma* species whose common host is the dog, cutaneous larval migrans affects humans, causing itching and lumps and streaks beneath the surface of the skin.

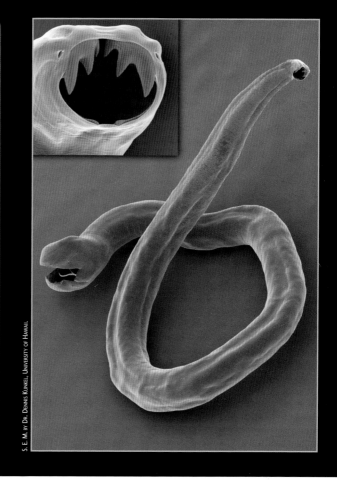

S. E. M. BY DR. DENNIS KUNKEL, UNIVERSITY OF HAWAII.

realize that bitches can pass ascarids to their pups even if they test negative prior to whelping. Accordingly, bitches are best treated at the same time as the pups.

HOOKWORMS

Unlike ascarids, hookworms do latch onto a dog's intestinal tract and can cause significant loss of blood and protein. Similar to ascarids, hookworms can be transmitted to humans, where they cause a condition known as cutaneous larval migrans. Dogs can become infected either by consuming the infective larvae or by the larvae's penetrating the skin directly. People most often get infected when they are lying on the ground (such as on a beach) and the larvae penetrate the skin. Yes, the larvae can penetrate through a beach blanket. Hookworms are typically susceptible to the same medications used to treat ascarids.

The hookworm *Ancylostoma caninum* infests the intestines of dogs. INSET: Note the row of hooks at the posterior end, used to anchor the worm to the intestinal wall.

WHIPWORMS

Whipworms latch onto the lower aspects of the dog's colon and can cause cramping and diarrhea. Eggs do not start to appear in the dog's feces until about three months after the dog was infected. This worm has a peculiar life cycle, which makes it more difficult to control than ascarids or hookworms. The good thing is that whipworms rarely are transferred to people.

Some of the medications used to treat ascarids and hookworms are also effective against whipworms, but, in general, a separate treatment protocol is needed. Since most of the medications are effective against the adults but not the eggs or larvae, treatment is typically repeated in three weeks, and then often in three

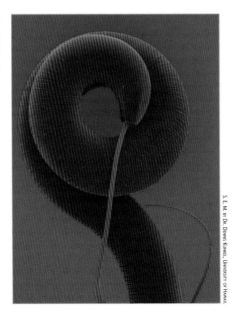

Adult whipworm, *Trichuris* sp., an intestinal parasite.

S. E. M. by Dr. Dennis Kunkel, University of Hawaii

WORM-CONTROL GUIDELINES

- Practice sanitary habits with your dog and home.
- Clean up after your dog and don't let him sniff or eat other dogs' droppings.
- Control insects and fleas in the dog's environment. Fleas, lice, cockroaches, beetles, mice and rats can act as hosts for various worms.
- Prevent dogs from eating uncooked meat, raw poultry and dead animals.
- Keep dogs and children from playing in sand and soil.
- Kennel dogs on cement or gravel; avoid dirt runs.
- Administer heartworm preventives regularly.
- Have your vet examine your dog's stools at your annual visits.
- Select a boarding kennel carefully so as to avoid contamination from other dogs or an unsanitary environment.
- Prevent dogs from roaming. Obey local leash laws.

months as well. Unfortunately, since dogs don't develop resistance to whipworms, it is difficult to prevent them from getting reinfected if they visit soil contaminated with whipworm eggs.

TAPEWORMS

There are many different species of tapeworm that affect dogs, but *Dipylidium caninum* is probably the most common and is spread by fleas. Flea larvae feed on organic debris and tapeworm eggs in the environment and, when a dog chews at himself and manages to ingest fleas, he might get a dose of tapeworm at the same time. The tapeworm then develops further in the intestine of the dog.

The tapeworm itself, which is a parasitic flatworm that latches onto the intestinal wall, is composed of numerous segments. When the segments break off into the intestine (as proglottids), they may accumulate around the rectum, like grains of rice. While this tapeworm is disgusting in its behavior, it is not directly communicable to humans (although humans can also get infected by swallowing fleas).

A much more dangerous tapeworm is *Echinococcus multilocularis*, which is typically found in foxes, coyotes and wolves. The eggs are passed in the feces and infect rodents, and, when dogs eat the rodents, the dogs can be infected by thousands of adult tapeworms. While the parasites don't cause many problems in dogs, this is considered the most lethal worm infection that people can get. Take appropriate precautions if you live in an area in which these tapeworms are found. Do not use mulch that may contain feces of dogs, cats or wildlife, and

discourage your pets from hunting wildlife. Treat these tapeworm infections aggressively in pets, because if humans get infected, approximately half die.

HEARTWORMS

Heartworm disease is caused by the parasite *Dirofilaria immitis* and is seen in dogs around the world. A member of the roundworm group, it is spread between dogs by the bite of an infected mosquito. The mosquito injects infective larvae into the dog's skin with its bite, and these larvae develop under the skin for a period of time before making their way to the heart. There they develop into adults, which grow and create blockages of the heart, lungs and major blood vessels there. They also start producing offspring (microfilariae),

S. E. M. BY DR. DENNIS KUNKEL, UNIVERSITY OF HAWAII.

A dog tapeworm proglottid (body segment).

S. E. M. BY DR. DENNIS KUNKEL, UNIVERSITY OF HAWAII.

The dog tapeworm *Taenia pisiformis*.

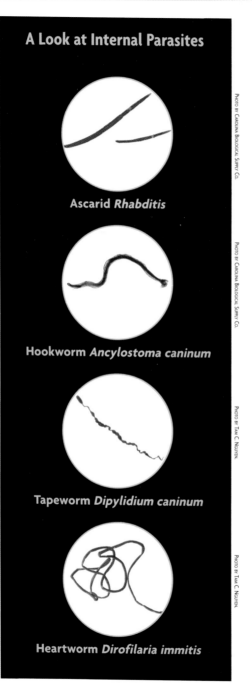

A Look at Internal Parasites

Ascarid *Rhabditis*

Hookworm *Ancylostoma caninum*

Tapeworm *Dipylidium caninum*

Heartworm *Dirofilaria immitis*

PHOTO BY CAROLINA BIOLOGICAL SUPPLY CO.

PHOTO BY CAROLINA BIOLOGICAL SUPPLY CO.

PHOTO BY TAM C. NGUYEN

PHOTO BY TAM C. NGUYEN

and these microfilariae circulate in the bloodstream, waiting to hitch a ride when the next mosquito bites. Once in the mosquito, the microfilariae develop into infective larvae and the entire process is repeated.

When dogs get infected with heartworm, over time they tend to develop symptoms associated with heart disease, such as coughing, exercise intolerance and potentially many other manifestations. Diagnosis is confirmed by either seeing the microfilariae themselves in blood samples or using immunologic tests (antigen testing) to identify the presence of adult heartworms. Since antigen tests measure the presence of adult heartworms and microfilarial tests measure offspring produced by adults, neither are positive until six to seven months after the initial infection. However, the beginning of damage can occur by fifth-stage larvae as early as three months after infection. Thus it is possible for dogs to be harboring problem-causing larvae for up to three months before either type of test would identify an infection.

The good news is that there are great protocols available for preventing heartworm in dogs. Testing is critical in the process, and it is important to understand the benefits as well as the limitations of such testing. All dogs six months of age or older that have not been on continuous heartworm-preventive medication should be

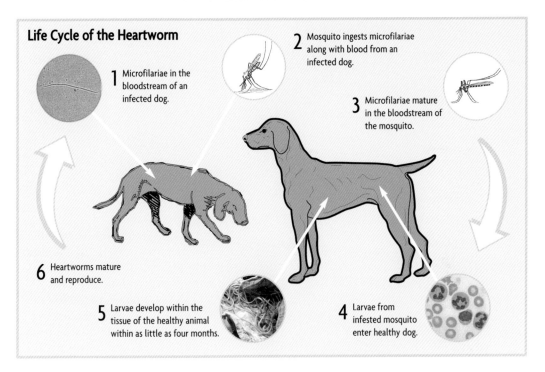

Life Cycle of the Heartworm

1 Microfilariae in the bloodstream of an infected dog.

2 Mosquito ingests microfilariae along with blood from an infected dog.

3 Microfilariae mature in the bloodstream of the mosquito.

4 Larvae from infested mosquito enter healthy dog.

5 Larvae develop within the tissue of the healthy animal within as little as four months.

6 Heartworms mature and reproduce.

screened with microfilarial or antigen tests. For dogs receiving preventive medication, periodic antigen testing helps assess the effectiveness of the preventives. The American Heartworm Society guidelines suggest that annual retesting may not be necessary when owners have absolutely provided continuous heartworm prevention. Retesting on a two- to three-year interval may be sufficient in these cases. However, your veterinarian will likely have specific guidelines under which heartworm preventives will be prescribed, and many prefer to err on the side of safety and retest annually.

It is indeed fortunate that heartworm is relatively easy to prevent, because treatments can be as life-threatening as the disease itself. Treatment requires a two-step process that kills the adult heartworms first and then the microfilariae. Prevention is obviously preferable; this involves a once-monthly oral or topical treatment. The most common oral preventives include ivermectin (not suitable for some breeds), moxidectin and milbemycin oxime; the once-a-month topical drug selamectin provides heartworm protection in addition to flea, some types of tick and other parasite controls.

SHOWING YOUR

GERMAN PINSCHER

Is dog showing in your blood? Are you excited by the idea of gaiting your handsome German Pinscher around the ring to the thunderous applause of an enthusiastic audience? Are you certain that your beloved German Pinscher is flawless? You are not alone! Every loving owner thinks that his dog has no faults, or too few to mention. No matter how many times an owner reads the breed standard, he cannot find any faults in his aristocratic companion dog. If this sounds like you, and if you are considering entering your German Pinscher in a dog show, here are some basic questions to ask yourself:

- Did you purchase a "show-quality" puppy from the breeder?
- Is your puppy at least six months of age?
- Does the puppy exhibit correct show type for his breed?
- Does your puppy have any disqualifying faults?
- Is your German Pinscher registered with a national kennel club?

- How much time do you have to devote to training, grooming, conditioning and exhibiting your dog?
- Do you understand the rules and regulations of a dog show?
- Do you have time to learn how to show your dog properly?
- Do you have the financial resources to invest in showing your dog?
- Will you show the dog yourself or hire a professional handler?
- Do you have a vehicle that can accommodate your weekend trips to the dog shows?

Success in the show ring requires more than a pretty face, a waggy tail and a pocketful of liver. Even though dog shows can be exciting and enjoyable, the sport of conformation makes great demands on the exhibitors and the dogs. Winning exhibitors live for their dogs, devoting time and money to their dogs' presentation, conditioning and training. Very few novices, even those with good dogs, will find themselves in the winners' circle, though it does happen. Don't be disheartened, though. Every exhibitor began as a novice and worked his way up to the Group ring. It's the "working your way up" part that you must keep in mind.

Assuming that you have purchased a puppy of the correct type and quality for showing, let's begin to examine the world of showing and what's required to get started. Although the entry fee into a dog show is nominal, there are lots of other hidden costs involved with "finishing" your German Pinscher, that is, making him a champion. Things like equipment, travel, training and conditioning all cost money. A more serious campaign will include fees for a professional handler, boarding, cross-country travel and advertising. Top-winning show dogs can represent a very considerable investment—over $100,000 has been spent in campaigning some dogs. (The investment can be less, of course, for owners who don't use professional handlers.)

Many owners, on the other hand, enter their "average" German Pinschers in dog shows for the fun and enjoyment of it. Dog showing makes an absorbing hobby, with many rewards for dogs and owners alike. If you're having fun, meeting other people who share your interests and enjoying the overall experience, you likely will catch the "bug." Once the dog-show bug bites, its effects can last a lifetime; it's

certainly much better than a deer tick! Soon you will be envisioning yourself in the center ring at the Westminster Kennel Club Dog Show in New York City, competing for the prestigious Best in Show cup. This magical dog show is televised annually from Madison Square Garden, and the victorious dog becomes a celebrity overnight.

German Pinschers in the ring at Westminster Kennel Club Dog Show 2005.

AKC CONFORMATION SHOWING

GETTING STARTED
Visiting a dog show as a spectator is a great place to start. Pick up the show catalog to find out what time your breed is being shown, who is judging the breed and in which ring the classes will be held. To start, German Pinschers compete against other German

Pinschers, and the winner is selected as Best of Breed by the judge. This is the procedure for each breed. At a group show, all of the Best of Breed winners go on to compete for Group One in their respective groups. For example, all Best of Breed winners in a given group compete against each other; this is done for all seven groups. Finally, all seven group winners go head to head in the ring for the Best in Show award.

What most spectators don't understand is the basic idea of conformation. A dog show is often referred to as a "conformation" show. This means that the judge should decide how each dog stacks up (conforms) to the breed standard for his given breed: how well does this German Pinscher conform to the ideal representative detailed in the standard? Ideally, this is what happens. In reality, however, this ideal often gets slighted as the judge compares German Pinscher #1 to German Pinscher #2. Again, the ideal is that each dog is judged based on his merits in comparison to his breed standard, not in comparison to the other dogs in the ring. It is easier for judges to compare dogs of the same breed to decide which they

Ch. Windamir's Vegas Des Charmettes, a 2005 national sweepstakes winner.

think is the better specimen; in the Group and Best in Show ring, however, it is very difficult to compare one breed to another, like apples to oranges. Thus the dog's conformation to the breed standard—not to mention advertising dollars and good handling—is essential to success in conformation shows. The dog described in the standard (the standard for each AKC breed is written and approved by the breed's national parent club and then submitted to the AKC for approval) is the perfect dog of that breed, and breeders keep their eye on the standard when they choose which dogs to breed, hoping to get closer and closer to the ideal with each litter.

A food reward will help a handler keep the dog's attention when in the ring.

Another good first step for the novice is to join a dog club. You will be astonished by the many and different kinds of dog clubs in the country, with about 5,000 clubs holding events every year. Most clubs require that prospective new members present two letters of recommendation from existing members. Perhaps you've made some friends visiting a show held by a particular club and you would like to join that club. Dog clubs may specialize in a single breed, like a local or regional German Pinscher club, or in a specific pursuit, such as obedience, tracking or hunting tests. There are all-breed clubs for all dog enthusiasts; they sponsor

special training days, seminars on topics like grooming or handling or lectures on breeding or canine genetics. There are also clubs that specialize in certain types of dogs, like herding dogs, hunting dogs, companion dogs, etc.

A parent club is the national organization, sanctioned by the national kennel club, which promotes and safeguards its breed in the country. The AKC parent club, the German Pinscher Club of America, was formed in 1985 and can be contacted on the Internet at www.german-pinscher.com. The parent club

Ch. Windamir Vogue Des Charmettes is more of the Schnauzer type of German Pinscher. Winning under judge Vic Clemente, owned by the authors.

which all AKC-recognized breeds can compete; the specialty show, which is for one breed only and usually sponsored by the breed's parent club and the group show, for all breeds in one of the AKC's seven groups. The German Pinscher competes in the Working Group.

For a dog to become an AKC champion of record, the dog must earn 15 points at shows. The points must be awarded by at least three different judges and must include two "majors" under different judges. A "major" is a three-, four- or five-point win, and the number of points per win is determined by the number of dogs competing in the show on that day. (Dogs that are absent or are excused are not counted.) The number of points that are awarded varies from breed to breed. More dogs are needed to attain a major in more popular breeds, and fewer dogs are needed in less popular breeds. Yearly, the AKC evaluates the number of dogs in competition in each division (there are 14 divisions in all, based on geography) and may or may not change the numbers of dogs required for each number of points.

Only one dog and one bitch of each breed can win points at a given show. There are no "co-ed" classes except for champions of record. Dogs and bitches do not compete against each other until

holds an annual national specialty show, usually in a different city each year, in which many of the country's top dogs, handlers and breeders gather to compete. At a specialty show, only members of a single breed are invited to participate. There are also group specialties, in which all members of a group are invited. For more information about dog clubs in your area, contact the AKC at www.akc.org on the Internet or write them at 5580 Centerview Drive, Raleigh, NC 27606.

How Shows Are Organized
Three kinds of conformation shows are offered by the AKC. There is the all-breed show, in

they are champions. Dogs that are not champions (referred to as "class dogs") compete in one of five classes. The class in which a dog is entered depends on age and previous show wins. First there is the Puppy Class (sometimes divided further into classes for 6- to 12-month-olds and 12- to 18-month-olds); next is the Novice Class (for dogs that have no points toward their championship and whose only first-place wins have come in the Puppy Class or the Novice Class, the latter class limited to three first places); then there is the American-bred Class (for dogs bred in the US); the Bred-by-Exhibitor Class (for dogs handled by their breeders or by immediate family members of their breeders); and the Open Class (for any non-champions). Any dog may enter the Open class, regardless of age or win history, but to be competitive the dog should be older and have ring experience.

The judge at the show begins judging the male dogs in the Puppy Class(es) and proceeds through the other classes. The judge awards first through fourth place in each class. The first-place winners of each class then compete with one another in the Winners Class to determine Winners Dog. The judge then starts over with the bitches, beginning with the Puppy Class(es) and proceeding up to the Winners Class to award Winners Bitch, just as he did with the dogs. A Reserve Winners Dog and Reserve Winners Bitch are also selected; they could be awarded the points in the case of a disqualification.

The Winners Dog and Winners Bitch are the two that are awarded the points for their breed. They then go on to compete with any champions of record (often called "specials") of their breed that are entered in the show. The champions may be dogs or bitches; in this class, all are shown together. The judge reviews the Winners Dog and Winners Bitch along with all of the champions to select the Best of Breed winner. The Best of Winners is selected between the Winners Dog and Winners Bitch;

Relaxing ringside at Crufts, England's largest dog show.

if one of these two is selected Best of Breed as well, he or she is automatically determined Best of Winners. Lastly, the judge selects Best of Opposite Sex to the Best of Breed winner. The Best of Breed winner then goes on to the group competition.

At a group or all-breed show, the Best of Breed winners from each breed are divided into their respective groups to compete against one another for Group One through Group Four. Group One (first place) is awarded to the dog that best lives up to the ideal for his breed as described in the standard. A group judge, therefore, must have a thorough working knowledge of many breed standards. After placements have been made in each group, the seven Group One winners (from the Working Group, Toy Group, Hound Group,

etc.) compete against each other for the top honor, Best in Show.

There are different ways to find out about dog shows in your area. The American Kennel Club's monthly magazine, the *American Kennel Gazette,* is accompanied by the *Events Calendar*; this magazine is available through subscription. You can also look on the AKC's and your parent club's websites for information and check the event listings in your local newspaper.

Your German Pinscher must be six months of age or older and registered with the AKC in order to be entered in AKC-sanctioned shows in which there are classes for the German Pinscher. Your German Pinscher also must not possess any disqualifying faults and must be sexually intact. The reason for the latter is simple: dog shows are the proving grounds to determine which dogs and bitches are worthy of being bred. If they cannot be bred, that defeats the purpose! On that note, only dogs that have achieved championships, thus proving their excellent quality, should be bred. If you have spayed or neutered your dog, however, there are many AKC events other than conformation, such as obedience trials, agility trials and the Canine Good Citizen® Program, in which you and your German Pinscher can participate.

Here is Ch. Windamir Roi Des Charmettes winning Best of Breed at the Monticello Kennel Club in 2003.

OTHER TYPES OF COMPETITION

In addition to conformation shows, the AKC holds a variety of other competitive events. Obedience trials, agility trials and tracking trials are open to all breeds, while hunting tests, field trials, lure-coursing, herding tests and trials, earthdog tests and coonhound events are limited to specific breeds or groups of breeds. The Junior Showmanship program is offered to aspiring young handlers and their dogs, and the Canine Good Citizen® Program is an all-around good-behavior test open to all dogs, pure-bred and mixed.

OBEDIENCE TRIALS

Mrs. Helen Whitehouse Walker, a Standard Poodle fancier, can be credited with introducing obedience trials to the United States. In the 1930s she designed a series of exercises based on those of the Associated Sheep, Police, Army Dog Society of Great Britain. These exercises were intended to evaluate the working relationship between dog and owner. Since those early days of the sport in the US, obedience trials have grown more and more popular, and now more than 2,000 trials each year attract over 100,000 dogs and their owners. Any dog registered with the AKC, regardless of neutering or other disqualifications that would

Ch. Windamir's Santa Des Charmettes is more of the Doberman type of German Pinscher. Owned by Sherwood Ingram.

preclude entry in conformation competition, can participate in obedience trials.

There are three levels of difficulty in obedience competition. The first (and easiest) level is the Novice, in which dogs can earn the Companion Dog (CD) title. The intermediate level is the Open level, in which the Companion Dog Excellent (CDX) title is awarded. The advanced level is the Utility level, in which dogs compete for the Utility Dog (UD) title. Classes at each level are further divided into "A" and "B," with "A" for beginners and "B" for those with more experience. In order to win a title at a given level, a dog must earn three "legs." A "leg" is accomplished when a dog scores 170 or higher (200 is a

Windamir's Hunter UD, the first UD German Pinscher in the US. Owned and trained by Georgia Welch.

addition, the dog must clear a broad jump, retrieve over a jump and drop on recall. In the Utility level, the exercises are quite difficult, including executing basic commands based on hand signals, following a complex heeling pattern, locating articles based on scent discrimination and completing jumps at the handler's direction.

Once he's earned the UD title, a dog can go on to win the prestigious title of Utility Dog Excellent (UDX) by winning "legs" in ten shows. Additionally, Utility Dogs who win "legs" in Open B and Utility B earn points toward the lofty title of Obedience Trial Champion (OTCh.). Established in 1977 by the AKC, this title requires a dog to earn 100 points as well as three first places in a combination of Open B and Utility B classes under three different judges. The "brass ring" of obedience competition is the AKC's National Obedience Invitational. This is an exclusive competition for only the cream of the obedience crop. In order to qualify for the invitational, a dog must be ranked in either the top 25 all-breeds in obedience or in the top three for his breed in obedience. The title at stake here is that of National Obedience Champion (NOC).

perfect score). The scoring system gets a little trickier when you understand that a dog must score more than 50% of the points available for each exercise in order to actually earn the points. Available points for each exercise range between 20 and 40.

A dog must complete different exercises at each level of obedience. The Novice exercises are the easiest, with the Open and finally the Utility levels progressing in difficulty. Examples of Novice exercises are on- and off-lead heeling, a figure-8 pattern, performing a recall (or come), long sit and long down and standing for examination. In the Open level, the Novice-level exercises are required again, but this time without a leash and for longer durations. In

AGILITY TRIALS
Agility trials became sanctioned by the AKC in August 1994, when the

first licensed agility trials were held. Since that time, agility certainly has grown in popularity by leaps and bounds, literally! The AKC allows all registered breeds (including Miscellaneous Class breeds) to participate, providing the dog is 12 months of age or older. Agility is designed so that the handler demonstrates how well the dog can work at his side. The handler directs his dog through, over, under and around an obstacle course that includes jumps, tires, the dog walk, weave poles, pipe tunnels, collapsed tunnels and more. While working his way through the course, the dog must keep one eye and ear on the handler and the rest of his body on the course. The handler runs along with the dog, giving verbal and hand signals to guide the dog through the course.

The first organization to promote agility trials in the US was the United States Dog Agility Association, Inc. (USDAA). Established in 1986, the USDAA sparked the formation of many member clubs around the country. To participate in USDAA trials, dogs must be at least 18 months of age.

The USDAA and AKC both offer titles to winning dogs, although the exercises and require-ments of the two organizations differ. Agility Dog (AD), Advanced Agility Dog (AAD) and Master Agility Dog (MAD) are the titles offered by the USDAA, while the AKC offers Novice Agility (NA), Open Agility (OA), Agility Excellent (AX) and Master Agility Excellent (MX). Beyond these four AKC titles, dogs can win additional titles in "jumper" classes: Jumper with Weave Novice (NAJ), Open (OAJ) and Excellent (MXJ). The ultimate title in AKC agility is MACH, Master Agility Champion. Dogs can continue to add number designations to the MACH title, indicating how many times the dog has met the title's requirements (MACH1, MACH2 and so on).

Agility trials are a great way to keep your dog active, and they will keep you running, too. You should join a local agility club to learn more about the sport. These clubs offer sessions in which you can introduce your dog to the various

Taking a leap into agility, Shooter makes this wing jump look easy.

It's a bird! It's a plane! No, it's Shooter, the German Pinscher agility dog.

obstacles as well as training classes to prepare him for competition. In no time, your dog will be climbing A-frames, crossing the dog walk and flying over hurdles, all with you right beside him. Your heart will leap every time your dog jumps through the hoop—and you'll be having just as much (if not more) fun!

TRACKING

Tracking tests are exciting ways to test your German Pinscher's instinctive scenting ability on a competitive level. All dogs have a nose, and all breeds are welcome in tracking tests. The first AKC-licensed tracking test took place in 1937 as part of the Utility level at an obedience trial, and thus competitive tracking was officially begun. The first title, Tracking Dog (TD), was offered in 1947, ten years after the first official tracking test. It was not until 1980 that the AKC added the title Tracking Dog Excellent (TDX), which was followed by the title Variable Surface Tracking (VST) in 1995. Champion Tracker (CT) is awarded to a dog who has earned all three of those titles.

The TD level is the first and most basic level in tracking,

Things are looking up for Shooter as he tackles the teeter exercise.

to try! Just as we have to choose what to do with our weekends, so do the dogs. Whatever you choose to do with your dog, it will take training, dedication and a willingness to work with your dog to achieve a common goal, a partnership between you and your dog. There is nothing more pleasing than to watch a handler and dog performing at a high level, whether it is in the show ring or the field. There is something for everyone and every dog in the world of dog "showing." Dog showing should really be called "competing with your dog." You are not restricted to the traditional "dog show" and may find that your "show dog" excels in other areas as well or instead.

Handsome, intelligent, athletic and versatile, German Pinschers are making their owners proud in many competitive venues.

Shooter demonstrates the tire exercise.

progressing in difficulty to the TDX and then the VST. A dog must follow a track laid by a human 30 to 120 minutes prior in order to earn the TD title. The track is about 500 yards long and contains up to 5 directional changes. At the next level, the TDX, the dog must follow a 3- to 5-hour-old track over a course that is up to 1,000 yards long and has up to 7 directional changes. In the most difficult level, the VST, the track is up to 5 hours old and located in an urban setting.

IN CONCLUSION
The bottom line is this: there is so much to do with your dog that it can be hard to decide which event

GERMAN PINSCHER

You chose your dog because something clicked the minute you set eyes on him. Or perhaps it seemed that the dog selected you and that's what clinched the deal. Either way, you are now investing time and money in this dog, a true pal and an outstanding member of the family. Everything about him is perfect—well, almost perfect. Remember, he is a dog! For that matter, how does he think *you're* doing?

UNDERSTANDING THE CANINE MINDSET

For starters, you and your dog are on different wavelengths. Your dog is similar to a toddler in that both live in the present tense only. A dog's view of life is based primarily on cause and effect. Your dog makes connections based on the fact that he lives in the present, so when he is doing something and you interrupt to dispense praise or a correction, a connection, positive or negative, is made. To the dog, that's like one plus one equals two! In the same sense, it's also easy to see that when your timing is off, you will cause an incorrect connection. The one-plus-one way of thinking is why you must never scold a dog for behavior that took place an hour, 15 minutes or even 5 seconds ago. But it is also why, when your timing is perfect, you can teach him to do all kinds of wonderful things—as soon as he has made that essential connection. What helps the process is his desire to please you and to have your approval.

There are behaviors we admire in dogs, such as friendliness and obedience, as well as those behaviors that cause problems to a varying degree. The dog owner who encounters minor behavioral problems is wise to

Part of understanding your dog is understanding his body language. This dog is saying, "I want to play!"

solve them promptly or get professional help. Bad behaviors are not corrected by repeatedly shouting "No" or getting angry with the dog. Only the giving of praise and approval for good behavior lets your dog understand right from wrong. The longer a bad behavior is allowed to continue, the harder it is to overcome. A responsible breeder is often able to help. Each dog is unique, so try not to compare your dog's behavior with your neighbor's dog or the one you had as a child.

Have your veterinarian check the dog to see whether a behavior problem could have a physical cause. An earache or toothache, for example, could be the reason for a dog to snap at you if you were to touch his head when putting on his leash. A sharp correction from you would only increase the behavior. When a physical basis is eliminated, and if the problem is not something you understand or can cope with, ask for the name of a behavioral specialist, preferably one who is familiar with the German Pinscher or similar breeds. Be sure to keep the breeder informed of your progress.

Many things, such as environment and inherited traits, form the basic behavior of a dog, just as in humans. You also must factor into his temperament the purpose for which your dog was originally bred. The major obstacle lies in

DOMINANCE

Dogs are born with dominance skills, meaning that they can be quite clever in trying to get their way. The "follow-me" trot to the cookie jar is an example. The toy dropped in your lap says "Play with me." The leash delivered to you along with an excited look means "Take me for a walk." These are all good-natured dominant behaviors. Ask your dog to sit before agreeing to his request and you'll remain "top dog."

the dog's inability to explain his behavior to us in a way that we understand. The one thing you should not do is to give up and abandon your dog. Somewhere a misunderstanding has occurred, but with help and patient understanding on your part, you should be able to work out the majority of bothersome behaviors.

AGGRESSION

"Aggression" is a word that is often misunderstood and is sometimes even used to describe what is actually normal canine behavior. For example, it's normal for puppies to growl when playing tug-of-war. It's puppy talk. There are different forms of dog aggression, but all are degrees of dominance, indicating that the dog, not his master, is (or thinks he is) in control. When the dog feels that he (or his control of the situation) is threatened, he will respond. The extent of the aggressive behavior varies with individual dogs. It is not at all pleasant to see bared teeth or to hear your dog growl or snarl, but these are signs of behavior that, if left uncorrected, can become extremely dangerous. A word of warning here: never challenge an aggressive dog. He is unpredictable and therefore unreliable to approach.

Nothing gets a "hello" from strangers on the street quicker than walking a puppy, but people should ask permission before petting your dog so you can tell him to sit in order to receive the admiring pats. If a hand comes down over the dog's head and he shrinks back, ask the person to bring their hand up, underneath the pup's chin. Now you're correcting strangers, too! But if you don't, it could make your dog afraid of strangers, which in turn can lead to fear-biting. Socialization prevents much aggression before it rears its ugly head.

The body language of an aggressive dog about to attack is clear. The dog will have a hard, steady stare. He will try to look as big as possible by standing stiff-legged, pushing out his chest, keeping his ears up and holding his tail up and steady. The hackles on his back will rise so that a ridge of hairs stands up. This posture may include the curled lip, snarl and/or growl or he may be silent. He looks, and definitely is, very dangerous.

This dominant posture is seen in dogs that are territorially aggressive. Deliverymen are constant victims of serious bites from such dogs. Territorial aggression is the reason you should never, ever try to train a puppy to be a watchdog. It can escalate into this type of behavior over which you will have no control. All forms of aggression must be taken seriously and dealt with immediately. If signs of aggressive behavior continue, or grow worse, or if you are at all unsure about how to deal with your dog's behavior, get the help of a professional.

Uncontrolled aggression, sometimes called "irritable aggres-

LEAD THE WAY

A dog that's becoming unreliable in his behavior needs to have his trust in your leadership reinforced. Are you being consistent, patient and fair? *Consistent* means that you are using the same words to expect the same response every time. *Patient* means that you haven't expressed the task clearly enough for your dog to understand, so you must persevere until you get the message across. *Fair* means that you see things from the dog's point of view. Angry words or physical punishment are unacceptable from a trusted leader.

sion," is not something for the pet owner to try to solve. If you cannot solve your dog's dangerous behavior with professional help, and you (quite rightly) do not wish to keep a canine time-bomb in your home, you will have some important decisions to make. Aggressive dogs often cannot be rehomed successfully, as they are dangerous and unreliable in their behavior. An aggressive dog should be dealt with only by someone who knows exactly the situation that he is getting into and has the experience, dedication and ideal living environment to attempt rehabilitating the dog, which often is not possible. In these cases, the dog ends up having to be humanely put down. Making a decision about euthanasia is not an easy undertaking for anyone, for any reason, but you cannot pass on to another home a dog that you know could cause harm.

A milder form of aggression is the dog's guarding anything that he perceives to be his—his food dish, his toys, his bed and/or his crate. This can be prevented if you take firm control from the start. The young puppy can and should be taught that his leader will share but that certain rules apply. Guarding is mild aggression only in the beginning stages, and it will worsen and become dangerous if you let it.

Don't try to snatch anything

Some dogs can become aggressive toward those who they perceive to invade their territory. Beware of warning signs and seek professional help if needed.

away from your puppy. Bargain for the item in question so that you can positively reinforce him when he gives it up. Punishment only results in worsening any aggressive behavior.

Many dogs extend their guarding impulse toward items they've stolen. The dog figures, "If I have it, it's mine"! (Some ill-behaved kids have similar tendencies.) An angry confrontation will only increase the dog's aggression. (Have you ever watched a child have a tantrum?) Try a simple distraction first, such as tossing a toy or picking up his leash for a walk. If that doesn't work, the best way to handle the situation is with basic obedience. Show the dog a treat, followed by calm, almost slow-motion commands: "Come. Sit. Drop it. Good dog," and then hand over the cheese! That's one example of positive-reinforcement training.

Children can be bitten when they try to retrieve a stolen shoe or toy, so they need to know how to handle the dog or to let an adult do it. They may also be bitten as they run away from a dog, in either fear or play. The dog sees the child's running as reason for pursuit, and even a friendly young puppy will nip at the heels of a runaway. Teach the kids not to run away from a strange dog and when to stop overly exciting play with their own puppy.

Fear biting is yet another aggressive behavior. A fear biter gives many warning signals. The dog leans away from the approaching person (sometimes hiding behind his owner) with his ears and tail down, but not in submission. He may even shiver. His hackles are raised, his lips curled. When the person steps into the dog's "flight zone" (a circle of 1 to 3 feet surrounding the dog), he attacks. Because of the fear factor, he performs a rapid attack-and-retreat. Because it is directed at a person, vets are often the victims of this form of aggression. It is frightening, but discovering and eliminating the cause of the fright will help overcome the dog's need to bite. Early socialization again plays a strong role in the prevention of this behavior. Again, if you can't cope with it, get the help of an expert.

If your dog has a tendency to take things he shouldn't, try offering something he can have as a distraction.

SEPARATION ANXIETY
Any behaviorist will tell you that separation anxiety is the most common problem about which pet owners complain. It is also one of the easiest to prevent. Unfortunately, a behaviorist usually is not consulted until the dog is a stressed-out, neurotic mess. At that stage, it is indeed a problem that requires the help of a professional.

Training the puppy to the fact that people in the house come and go is essential in order to avoid this anxiety. Leaving the puppy in his crate or a confined area while family members go in and out, and stay out for longer and longer periods of time, is the basic way to desensitize the pup to the family's frequent departures. If you are at home most of every day, make it a point to go out for at least an hour or two whenever possible.

How you leave is vital to the dog's reaction. Your dog is no fool. He knows the difference between sweats and business suits, jeans and dresses. He sees you pat your pocket to check for your wallet, open your briefcase, check that you have your cell phone or pick up the car keys. He knows from the hurry of the kids in the morning that they're off to school until afternoon. Lipstick? Aftershave lotion? Lunch boxes? Every move you make registers in his sensory perception and memory. Your puppy knows more about your departures than you do. You can't get away with a thing!

Before you got dressed, you checked the dog's water bowl and his supply of long-lasting chew toys and turned the radio on low. You will leave him in what he considers his "safe" area, not with total freedom of the house. If you've invested in child safety gates, you can be reasonably sure that he'll remain in the designated area. Don't give him access to a window where he can watch you leave the house. If you're leaving for an hour or two, put him into his crate with a safe toy.

Now comes the test. You are ready to walk out the door. Do not give your German Pinscher a big hug and a fond farewell. Do not drag out a long goodbye. Those are the very things that jump-start separation anxiety. Toss a biscuit into the dog's area, call out "So long, Fritzy" and close the door. You're gone. The chances are that the dog may bark a couple of times, or maybe whine once or twice, and then settle down to enjoy his biscuit and take a lovely nap, especially if you took him for a nice long walk before leaving. As he grows up, the barks and whines will stop because it's an old routine, so why should he make the effort?

When you first brought home the puppy, the come-and-go routine was intermittent and constant. He was put into his crate with a tiny treat. You left (silently) and returned in 3 minutes, then 5, then 10, then 15, then half an hour, until finally you could leave without a problem and be gone for 2 or 3 hours. If, at any time in the future, there's a "separation" problem, refresh his memory by going back to that basic training.

Now comes the next most important part—your return. Do not make a big production of coming home. "Hi, Fritzy" is as grand a greeting as he needs. When you've taken off your hat and coat, tossed your briefcase on the hall table and glanced at the mail, and the dog has settled down from the excitement of seeing you "in person" from his confined area, then go and give him a warm, friendly greeting. A potty trip is needed and a walk would be appreciated, since he's been such a good dog.

MATTERS OF SEX

For whatever reasons, real or imagined, most people tend to have a preference in choosing between a male and female puppy. Some, but not all, of the undesirable traits attributed to the sex of the dog can be suppressed by early spaying or neutering. The major advantage, of course, is that a neutered male or a spayed female will not be adding to the overpopulation of dogs.

An unaltered male will mark territory by lifting his leg everywhere, leaving a few drops of urine indoors on your furniture and appliances and outside on everything he passes. It is difficult to catch him in the act, because he leaves only a few drops each time, but it is very hard to eliminate the odor. Thus the cycle begins, because the odor will entice him to mark that spot again.

If you have bought a bitch with the intention of breeding her, be sure you know what you are getting into. She will go through one or two periods of estrus each year, each cycle lasting about three weeks. During those times she will have to be kept confined to protect your furniture and to protect her from being bred by a male other than the one you have selected. Breeding should never be undertaken to "show the kids the miracle of birth." Bitches can die giving birth, and the puppies may also die. The dam often exhibits what is called "maternal aggression" after the pups are born. Her intention is to protect her pups, but in fact she can act quite vicious. Breeding should be left to the experienced breeders, who do so for the betterment of the breed and with much research and planning behind each mating.

Mounting is not unusual in dogs, male or female. Puppies do it to each other and adults do it regardless of sex, because it is not so much a sexual act as it is one of dominance. It becomes very annoying when the dog mounts your legs, the kids or the couch cushions; in these and any other instances of mounting, he should be corrected. Touching sometimes stimulates the dog, so pulling the dog off by his collar or leash, together with a consistent and stern "Off!" command, usually eliminates the behavior.

CHEWING

All puppies chew. All adult dogs chew. This is a fact of life for canines, and sometimes you may think it's what your dog does best! A pup starts chewing when his first set of teeth erupts and continues throughout the teething period. Chewing gives the pup relief from itchy gums and incoming teeth, and from that time on, he gets great satisfaction out of this normal, somewhat idle, canine activity. Providing safe chew toys is the best way to direct this behavior in an appropriate manner. Chew toys are available in all sizes, textures and flavors, but you must monitor the wear-and-tear inflicted on your pup's toys to be sure that the ones you've chosen are safe and remain in good condition.

Puppies cannot distinguish between a rawhide toy and a nice leather shoe or wallet. It's up to you to keep your possessions away from the dog and to keep your eye on the dog. There's a form of destruction caused by chewing that is not the dog's fault. Let's say you allow him on the sofa. One day he takes a chew bone up on the sofa and, in the course of chewing on the bone, takes up a bit of fabric. He continues to chew. Disaster! Now you've learned the lesson: dogs with chew toys have to be either kept off furniture and carpets, carefully supervised or put into their confined areas for chew time.

The wooden legs of furniture are favorite objects for chewing.

> ### ONE BITE TOO MANY
> It's natural for puppies to bite in play, but you must teach your puppy that this is unacceptable in human circles. Relax your hand, say "No bite" and offer him a toy. An adolescent dog is testing his dominance and will bite as a way of disobeying you. If not stopped in puppyhood, you will end up with an adult dog that will bite aggressively. All adult biting should be considered serious and dealt with by a professional.

The first time, tell the dog "Leave it!" (or "No!") and offer him a chew toy as a substitute. However, your clever dog may be hiding under the chair and doing some silent destruction, which you may not notice until it's too late. In this case, it's time to try one of the foul-tasting products, made specifically to prevent destructive chewing, that is sprayed on the objects of your dog's chewing attention. These products also work to keep the dog away from plants, trash, etc. It's even a good way to stop the dog from "mouthing" or chewing on your hands or the leg of your pants. (Be sure to wash your hands after the mouthing lesson!) A little spray goes a long way.

DIGGING
Digging is another natural and normal doggie behavior. Wild canines dig to bury whatever food

they can save for later to eat.
(And you thought *we* invented
the doggie bag!) Burying bones or
toys is a primary cause to dig.
Dogs also dig to get at interesting
little underground creatures like
moles and mice. In the summer,
they dig to get down to cool
earth. In winter, they dig to get
beneath the cold surface to
warmer earth. To understand how
natural and normal this is you
have only to consider the Nordic
breeds of sled dog who, at the
end of the run, routinely dig a
bed for themselves in the snow.

> **CURES FOR COMMON BOREDOM**
>
> Dogs are social animals that need company. Lonely and tied-out dogs bark, hoping that someone will hear them. Prevent this from happening by never tying your dog out in the yard and by giving him the attention that he needs. If you don't, then don't blame the dog. Bored dogs will think up clever ways to overcome their boredom. Digging is a common diversion for a dog left alone outside for too long. The remedy is to bring him indoors or put a layer of crushed stone in his confined outdoor area. If you catch him in the act of "gardening," it requires immediate correction. Keep your dog safe by embedding the fencing a foot or more below ground level to foil a would-be escape artist.

It's the nesting instinct. How
often have you seen your dog go
round and round in circles,
pawing at his blanket or bedding
before flopping down to sleep?

Domesticated dogs also dig to
escape, and that's a lot more
dangerous than it is destructive. A
dog that digs under the fence is
the one that is hit by a car or
becomes lost. A good fence to
protect a digger should be set 12
inches below ground level, and
every fence needs to be routinely
checked for even the smallest
openings that can become possible
escape routes.

Catching your dog in the act of
digging is the easiest way to stop
it, because your dog will make the
"one-plus-one" connection, but
digging is too often a solitary
occupation, something the lonely
dog does out of boredom. Catch
your puppy in the act and put a
stop to it before you have a yard
full of craters. It is more difficult
to stop if your dog sees you
gardening. If you can dig, why
can't he? Because you say so,
that's why! Some dogs are excava-
tion experts, and some dogs never
dig. However, when it comes to
any of these instinctive canine
behaviors, never say "never."

FOOD-RELATED PROBLEMS
We're not talking about eating,
diets or nutrition here, we're
talking about bad habits. Face it.
All dogs are beggars. Food is the

DOGS OF PREY
Chasing small animals is in the blood of many dogs, perhaps most; they think that this is a fun recreational activity (although some are more likely to bring you an undesirable "gift" as a result of the hunt). The good old "Leave it" command works to deter your dog from taking off in pursuit of "prey," but only if taught with the dog on leash for control.

motivation for everything we want our dogs to do and, when you combine that with their innate ability to "con" us in order to get their way, it's a wonder there aren't far more obese dogs in the world.

Who can resist the bleeding-heart look that says "I'm starving," or the paw that gently pats your knee or a perfect sit beneath the cookie jar. No one who professes to love his dog can turn down the pleas of his clever canine's performances every time. One thing is for sure, though: definitely do not allow begging at the table. Family meals do not include your dog.

Control your dog's begging habit by making your dog work for his rewards. Ignore his begging when you can. Utilize the obedience commands you've taught your dog. His reward in these situations is definitely not a treat! Casual verbal praise is enough. Be sure all members of the family follow the same rules.

There is a different type of begging that does demand your immediate response and that is the appeal to be let (or taken) outside! Usually that is a quick paw or small whine to get your attention, followed by a race to the door. This type of begging needs your quick attention and approval.

Stealing food is a problem only if you are not paying attention. A dog can't steal food that is not within his reach. Leaving your dog in the kitchen with the roast beef on the table is asking for trouble. Putting cheese and crackers on the coffee table also requires a watchful eye to stop the thief in his tracks. The word to use (one word, remember, even if it's two words pronounced as one) is "Leave it!" Instead of preceding it with yet another "No," try using a guttural sound like "Aagh!" That sounds more like a warning growl to the dog and therefore has instant meaning.

Your dog will think he's been exceptionally clever if he causes a child to drop a cookie. Bonanza! The easiest solution is to keep dog and children separated at snack time. You must also be sure that the children understand that they must not tease the dog with food—his or theirs. Your dog does not mean to bite the kids, but when he snatches at a tidbit so near the level of his mouth, it can result in an unintended nip.

INDEX

Page numbers in **boldface** indicate illustrations.

My German Pinscher

PUT YOUR PUPPY'S FIRST PICTURE HERE

Dog's Name _____

Date _____ Photographer _____